One Hundred Answers
from Spirit

Also by Gordon Smith:

The Best of Both Worlds

GORDON SMITH

One Hundred Answers from Spirit

Britain's greatest medium answers
the great questions of life and death

CORONET

First published in Great Britain in 2016 by Coronet
An imprint of Hodder & Stoughton
An Hachette UK company

1

A CIP catalogue record for this title is available
from the British Library

Hardback ISBN: 978 1 444 79087 0
Ebook ISBN: 978 1 444 79088 7

Typeset in Plantin Light by Palimpsest Book Production Limited,
Falkirk, Stirlingshire

Printed and bound by Clays Ltd, St Ives plc

Ho   natural,
rene   rown
in su   esses
are e   of the

Contents

Contents

Foreword

Throughout the twenty-odd years of my work as a medium I have had the wonderful opportunity to help many, many people cope with their grief and get a fresh, positive outlook on life. There must be many thousands who have come to live demonstrations and received messages from their loved ones from the other side; giving them evidence that their spirit has survived after, what we know as, physical death.

What most of these people do not know is that my work as a medium began in a very different way and has developed over the years to become a very different kind of mediumship, not often shared with the public. This other form of mediumship is called 'trance mediumship'. In this form, the medium goes into a much deeper, altered state of consciousness or trance, and allows the spirit guide, or indeed guides, to come and use his or her voice to communicate directly with people in this world.

The trance mediumship that I developed over the years was only ever used for the people who sat with me in my own private development group. It was always treated by us as a guide to our progression; to learn more about mediumship and the spirit world, and further our spiritual development.

But it so happened that people in the spiritualist churches, where I mostly worked then, would hear of some of the philosophy that was coming through from the spirit world and would ask if I could hold a session for their own private groups and people within their inner circles. This began to happen more often in these private gatherings and it has continued, on and off, now for more than twenty years, and in that time thousands of questions have been answered by the spirit guides on varying subjects which affect our life. Trance is a part of my life as a medium that I have allowed to be used only for those on the spiritual path, but more recently it would seem that more and more people are becoming interested in this type of mediumship and the higher teachings that come with it.

In the course of this work many people from all different walks of life have put forth questions on a wide range of topics, covering more or less the whole human experience. So I have collected many of the answers which Spirit have given from transcripts and taped recordings of the sessions over the years and put them to good use as teachings.

For years these teachings have been in my possession, but I never really did anything about them. Sure, some of the answers are in some of the other books I have written, but so far there has been no book of answers from Spirit standing on its own. Now I feel that the time has come to offer yet another tool to people searching for answers, especially as, for reasons of time, I cannot offer private sessions anymore and even the events I take part in are limited.

It has been the way with all the books I have written; just when I have an idea about something, I get a confirmation from one source or another that proves for me that the time is right to begin writing. With this book I had that same confirmation when I was giving a talk to an audience of about a hundred people and a lady approached to ask me, 'Gordon, why don't you write a book with frequently asked questions and answers by Spirit?'

I smiled and told her, 'Well, dear lady, you might not believe it, but that is exactly what I am doing right now.' I did not tell her that earlier that week I had been approached by a publisher to do just that.

But I did find it a little bit funny as it was the first time that anyone had asked me to publish a book with answers by Spirit. That shows how the synchronicity of the spiritual world works, once we are open to be in tune with it.

Actually, now more than ever before in history, people are taxed by the challenges of *modern* life, almost to their max. Many then tend to lose their focus on what they really want from life: how they really want to live, what goals are worthwhile to pursue, and which talents of theirs are calling to be realized.

Most of all, how they can take charge of their own life again, much more fully than before; how they can develop personal accountability and spiritual awakening, how they can manifest more of who they really are.

These are a few of the decisive reasons why this book came into existence. However, it is important to understand one very important aspect of any answer by Spirit to any question: answers are all well and good as long as they help you, as long as they build you up and remind you of both your own spiritual essence and your sovereignty.

If any answers – by Spirit, by a counsellor, by a therapist, a guru, a church person or anyone else – start to turn into dogmas, into iron fetters that confine you, then discard them. Do not accept them any longer. This is what my spirit guides made very clear when they agreed to help the readers, and myself, with this book.

During the course of this book, answers came from several evolved spirits, but mostly from my own spirit guide who I call Master Chi or, in some cases, just Chi. This is not his exact name, but it is what we use for the purpose of the trance sessions. All of the answers which were given were done so as direct responses to direct questions put to him by different individuals who attended the sessions. All the while my conscious mind was in a deep trance state and was not, to my knowledge, affecting any of the answers that came through. I hope you will realize the difference in personality between my offerings in this book and that of Chi and the other spirit guides, who have a much higher perspective of life than I ever could. So, with all that in mind, please read, enjoy and utilize this book in this very spirit: as a direct and useful link to Spirit for your own life!

I

The Human Journey

Introduction

Throughout my life working as a medium and travelling to many countries around the world I have encountered hundreds, if not thousands, of questions from people asking about their lives and why certain things happen to them when not to others. It has always been my own opinion that each person will have a different perspective on life and therefore the answers I give are always based on what I feel would benefit that particular person at that particular moment; as a medium I get a sense of what they need within the question they ask, and often in the way they ask it.

For example, two different people might ask me if there is some sort of punishment for people on the other side if they have done bad things in this life. One person may ask this question because they have been wronged by someone who is now in the spirit world and want to hear of retribution; whereas another might have a loved one in the spirit world who lived a life that was not so good, but they loved them and hope that there is some system of forgiveness over there.

It is often difficult in such situations to remain diplomatic with the questioner because if you do not truly know their emotional state when they ask such things, the answer you give might offend.

So I am as interested as anyone else to hear the answers which come through from my spirit guide Master Chi, or other guides, when I give a trance session to people. More often than not, he seems to touch the very core of the person who puts the question to him as the higher spirit mind knows what will truly benefit the individual, but the answer will also have the same effect on all other people in a way they need to understand it.

Master Chi is a spirit being whom I first recognized through my work as a medium in my mid-twenties. It is common for mediums to sense a guiding figure around them when they are in development; if you like, they are the unseen teachers and guardians who direct the medium and who assist their work from the spirit world.

Chi first appeared to me in a meditation as a very humble Asian man and I have always visualized him as a loner in nature, as most of his later teachings suggest that in his human existence he learned much from the natural world. Though I have never found official records of his life, he has many times given me places and times in history when he walked the physical world, and all have checked out.

For me, my guide represents a higher intelligence, a spiritual mind that is much more evolved than my own, but who can use my mind and body to channel relevant intelligent facts and information. I see him as the voice of Spirit – a bridge between higher and lower mind and a great guiding light for my own life.

The following questions have come from several sessions with my guide where the questions referred to the journey through human life.

What is the true purpose of each human life?

The purpose of human existence is quite simply to grow and learn from the experience of the situations which you face during your lifetime. If you take a moment to consider how far the understanding and behaviour of man has grown from first existing in this world, you will have something to measure the movement and progression of his journey from then till now. Also, if you consider the human world just now and all the negatives that can be worked on to bring about a more spiritual, stable existence, you may have more of an idea how much has still to be experienced and learned to further man's progression.

Why do some people get harder lives than others?

This comes from the very beginning of man's existence in this world. Some managed to easily achieve the lessons put in front of them while others struggled; all things that followed were unbalanced because of the law of cause and effect which governs man's actions and thus lessons were created from the acts of good and bad actions and right and wrong actions. With each new age of man in this world there come realizations which bring clarity, and where you are at this moment is on the edge of the dawning of a new realization, which will cause great effect in bringing about more balance.

Never assume that, in human terms, much can be achieved in this one lifetime. No, regard yourself fortunate when you recognize those who struggle more than you do through this life. And strive to reach the heights of those you feel are more fortunate than you. Remember, you alone cannot bring complete balance to the problems of the human world, but you can achieve balance in the one life you are in control of.

Is suffering really what makes us grow spiritually and, if so, why?

No one will grow from struggling if they are not able to see it from a higher perspective. But when you realize that the difficult times are what make you stop and wake up from the otherwise automatic flow of living in the human world, and cause you to consider your existence and ask questions, then you can understand more that the suffering in your life is more of a lesson than a punishment.

This is a system of growth that will expand your conscious mind and allow you to change how you view your experiences in your life. To struggle and resist change out of ignorance . . . then nothing much around you will ever change.

Is there a karmic balance in our human journey? Like if we get something good in our life, will we then have to experience something bad to achieve balance?

There are times when one, as you call it, good experience will follow a bad one, but it is not a natural law for this to be exact. There are times when one good action can change a life till its conclusion; just as another action may bring about a stream of disastrous events to the point of human death.

But try to understand that to balance good and bad does not always bring perfect balance in a life, there are other things to consider which have scales of polarity, and other aspects of the human life to consider before true balance is struck.

For you, may I say it would be better to look for contentment in the midst of all things in your life which are deemed to be good and bad? Remember, the contented mind has more chance of finding balance than that which moves up and down.

Is there any difference in the spirit world between people who have lived good lives from those who chose to be bad?

I would have to say that conscience is one immediate difference. If the man who has chosen to live a good life, but was doing so to escape difficult experiences which could have caused his mind to expand and grow, then his conscience on returning to the spirit world may become heavier because of this.

In the case of the man who has chosen to live a life filled with bad actions, which caused ill effect on himself and others, then he will surely be faced with a weight of conscience he has created for himself which will in turn restrict his own spiritual progression.

But if he is ignorant to all of his actions because he has no awareness of what he has previously done to himself or others, then the weight of his conscience will not allow him to gravitate to any spiritual level in the spirit world and the density of his consciousness will cause him to manifest in the lowest form through his complete ignorance.

Is there a heaven and hell?

If you choose to create either it will exist. In all aspects of life there are states of being; that which you call heaven is understood to be a reward for being good, whereas the hell you ask about is a place of punishment, is it not? Both reward and punishment are experienced in the human mind and there to remind you of good and bad.

Like most things considered by the human mind, they have opposites and not much understanding of middle. If you choose to create one, the other will exist as its opposite whether you want it to or not. It is much better to be centred and accepting of your highs and lows, as only from the centre can you truly affect balance.

If a baby dies, is that because they do not need to experience too much of the physical life?

There are times when a certain consciousness needs only to touch the human world and return; in some occasions it is all that they require to experience of the physical world. For those in the human world this is felt as emotional pain and grief, but such emotional experiences are not to be seen as punishment, but a contract between all concerned. It is in such a contract that you are given opportunities to experience different emotional situations as part

of the human journey you are moving through at
the time.

Can we change our path in this life? And how can we do that?

The opportunity to change is part of the contract
you have made before you come into this world and
to find the correct elements, which will change your
direction, are what constitute a successful life over
a failed life. All of you will find that there are times
and situations on your journey that will present themselves to you.

You may find that these are the times when you
have to act alone and take responsibility for the action
you are about to make. These are the times when it
is most easy to change the direction of your path,
but almost always there is a heavy burden of fear
which accompanies the moments when the human
mind must take control of the human journey.

Again I say that such times when fear enters into
your mind at the most important moments of your
life, this is when you must allow yourself to act as
spontaneously as possible; for your higher consciousness knows what will happen no matter what road
you follow, but your human mind will doubt, because
it reacts to fear more than trust. You may only have
a few such moments in your human life, so remember,
trust what you feel at the centre of you, not what
you hear in your fear-filled thoughts.

If we learn what we came here to learn, then does that mean we do not have to come again?

You never had to come in the first place; this entire journey is one you have chosen to follow. The problem for the human mind is that it is not in the position, while limited to a physical body with limited senses and memory, to remember its condition in the spirit world; this is where you come from and will always return.

The human journey is such a small part of your existence and to the spirit mind it is but a moment without clarity. On returning to your spiritual home, you will no doubt understand much more than you do now, but in the meantime just know that the lifetime you spend in the physical world is a tiny transition when measured against eternity.

What would be the best advice you could give to someone who wants to improve his or her life and become more spiritual?

Try to become more mindful and observant of your actions in the physical world. Learn to fear less the situations you find yourself in and know without doubt that everything will change. Remember to try to be compassionate on your journey and experience love as much as you can as it will remind you where you have come from.

Summary

Going over these answers given by Chi, it shows me that he speaks from his place of certainty much more than I do when I am faced with the same types of question; this highlights how beyond emotions Spirit are from us in the human world.

In another session Chi was asked a very personal question from a woman who had suffered the loss of all her family, leaving her as the sole remaining member alone in this world: why, if we all have choice, did they all choose to leave her? His answer was simple, he told her, 'in the same way you chose to remain without them'.

Many of the other sitters in the group felt this answer was cold, but Chi obviously sensed this reaction and continued to tell the entire group that as long as they felt like victims in this world, then nothing would be accomplished. He reminded them that true compassion was often harsh, but the more stern side of compassion was the one people learned from the most.

He then told the lady to look for the things that she still wanted to accomplish in her life and the reason for her outliving the rest of her family would become clear. At this the lady told him she wasn't sure where her life was going, to which Chi came back as quick as a flash saying that she was carrying in her bag a ticket to travel to America, which was her long-time dream, and that during this trip she would get more clarity on the latest episode of her life.

The lady agreed and was shocked to know that my guide knew what she had in her bag, as she had told no one at the session. Something in this action brought a spark into her eyes; maybe it was because he did something a little more phenomenal, or maybe he just reminded her that there would be life for her after all the loss she had experienced. Whatever it was, this lady seemed to shine more than anyone else at the end of the session. I believe he just renewed her hope.

2

Birth, Predestiny and Other Lives

Introduction

As a medium I am constantly asked questions about past lives and predestiny. I always do my best to answer what I believe, and anything that I have experienced in my own life can sometimes help, like when I first went to France as a teenager with my uncle on a day visit to Dieppe.

On arriving at the port, my uncle asked me if I wanted to go and buy some gifts first, and he headed off in the same direction as the crowd that had disembarked the boat. I called out to him that he was going the wrong way. His reaction was one of shock, especially when I told him the names of streets and places we should visit while we were there.

Even though I had never travelled to France in my whole life, it felt, to me, like I had been in this place before. The other confusing thing for my uncle was that we were actually planning to visit a different port that morning, but due to heavy traffic on the road we had missed the crossing, so he knew I'd had no way of researching the town of Dieppe. Until that morning I had never even heard of it.

I honestly do not know if I lived there in a previous life, but what I experienced that day was quite over-whelming and it left me feeling quite disorientated. As well as knowing the street names before we walked around a particular corner, I also remembered bars and cafés, which I felt I had been in before. As I say, I do not know if it was something to do with my own psychic abilities or if something in me returned to a previous time, but something out of the ordinary definitely happened to me on that day. I was fifteen then and nothing since has ever come to me about a life in France, or in fact Dieppe, but my mind remains open and as long as it does, then who knows?

Is our life predestined or do we have choices?

In every aspect of life there is always free will and the opportunity to make choices. But there is also an element of predestiny in each human incarnation that the higher consciousness makes.

If we look at the human incarnation as a journey, then you can imagine that before you set out on any journey there is an element of planning involved. What you must learn here is that there are options you will give yourself, which could determine different paths that will in turn create different endings to your journey.

So if we call these paths *timelines* then it might make it clearer to you when you look at the life you are in at this moment. I'm certain that you will have come to points in your life when you have had to make a choice to move in one direction or another.

The moment you acted on your choice you will have directed yourself onto a particular timeline, which will have had a different outcome to your life than if your choice had taken you on the alternative path. So this should make it a bit more clear to you that when you are faced with a major decision regarding change in your life, you are carrying out free will within the structure of predestiny.

Have you never known of a person in your world that has turned their life around against all odds and become what seems like a completely new person? Such an event may possibly be termed in your world as an act of God; I say to you that it is not, but more an act of self, because he has in fact changed his timeline, something he put in his plan before he entered the human incarnation.

Do we choose our parents and where we will be born?

In the case of one who has the awareness to do so, this is the case. It may all seem confusing to you at this point from the human perspective, but with the Spirit overview it is clear. The impending incarnation is worked out at a much higher level of consciousness between all involved in the future journey; the relationships and interactions which the travelling consciousness needs to experience.

Again, I say to you that this may all seem very confusing to you, and if it does then leave such wondering alone until it sits well with your mind. There are times when I cannot give too much information on this subject because to confuse the human mind would not serve any great purpose and this is why so much of your spirit life is left behind when you enter into the human life.

Remember, in the physical form your capacity for spiritual knowledge is limited, so always only accept what you can and what serves you well and leave what confuses you alone.

When does the spirit begin its journey into the physical world – at conception or at birth?

Is it not already clear to you in this more advanced time that the life of the growing child can be measured by medical instrument as it develops within the mother's womb? The contract of the human journey is made before conception, but the life-force makes its first contact with the future parents in the very moment of conception.

During the act of mating, all living physical beings give off what can best be described as an electrical emission, which, when the moment is correct, can allow the waiting consciousness to fuse or bond with the chemicals of the mating adults.

For you it might be difficult to visualize life forming within a much finer essence of life, but for the spirit it is much closer to what we are at this more subtle state of being. Try to imagine for a moment what the wind would look like if you could see it with your eyes, when, in your reality, you cannot actually see the force of air moving.

No, you only recognize its force when it moves through something more solid like grass, or water, or the leaves on the trees, but to your sight it cannot actually be seen. What I am saying to you at this time is that there are forces and even chemical workings active all around you in a much more subtle atmosphere every moment of your life.

Is there a time when consciousness switches on? And if so, when is that?

Consciousness is always, as you say, 'switched on'; in the way you ask the question it would seem that you still don't understand the nature of the thing you ask about. Try to consider that consciousness is ever active, ever moving and ever changing. It is always moving forward and constantly expanding.

The part of you which is conscious right now could only be compared to a particle of water within a vast ocean, just as the tiny particle cannot comprehend the scale of what it is part of, neither can you fathom the vastness of consciousness you are part of in its entirety. In your question it would appear that you are asking about an individual consciousness, but like the smallest particle of the ocean, though it can be isolated and examined as such, nevertheless it is still part of an unmeasurable source.

In your human form you tend to look at all things from the individual perspective and this is understandable, but when looking at such a subject as consciousness it is difficult to divide or dissect it as it is a whole, an entirety with countless numbers of components, of which you are but one.

From the spirit's point of view, what happens and what does it feel like to be born?

In your question you have asked how it feels; this makes it quite personal and it would be difficult to be accurate, but if I give you a more general account this may be of some use to you. Try to imagine that the consciousness is like air. As the air particles fuse together there is a reaction, which causes heat and attracts vapour that begins to continue the process of density forming.

So now the consciousness is not so fine, not so subtle, and what was once free to expand is becoming more confined within a structure. At a point the liquid begins to solidify and eventually becomes physical in the form of human cells. With each chemical reaction the once unlimited mind is condensing and becoming more physical.

The mind that was connected to all knowledge is becoming narrower and forgetful of its own vastness. It concentrates all its efforts on forming a self in physical form and, as the human self begins to develop, the spiritual self becomes like a thread of light; its lifeline to the formless world from where it began its journey.

You may recognize the silver cord, which people who have had an experience of near-death relate to; this is the source of your spiritual energy and, though undetected in the human world, is what feeds your conscious mind even now.

As for the individual birth process, I cannot say what each child experiences during its commencement into the human world. I myself cannot remember what it felt like in my last incarnation to the physical world.

Are there ever any times when people remember their spirit life or past life and if so, why does this happen, and what effect does it have or what purpose?

There are times when memories are brought from one lifetime into another, but in most cases the previous-life memories are stored in the higher conscious mind, which is ever present in the spirit world.

If on the occasion that a human incarnation did

not end well, or if there was much fear experienced in that particular life, then the consciousness would want to refine and try to experience similar challenges in the next incarnation in order to make more sense and understand the experiences more. It may be part of the plan it has given to itself to remember moments from before as a means to facing them again with more direction or as a challenge to overcome them.

Even though in the human world such things as remembering moments from a previous existence would be deemed as impossible to some, for the one who experiences such happenings it feels very real, and in some cases very frightening. This may be one effect: to be frightened because one has had a sense of something not considered to be normal to the human mind, but it would also have been part of that life plan to do so. If this is the case, then the purpose would have been to bring knowledge of previous existences in order to inform the human self that such a thing is possible. You will find that this type of phenomenon will occur more and more as your world begins to open and become more spiritual in its evolution.

Do we really reincarnate from one life to the other or is there time spent in the spirit world between lives?

It is difficult for you to understand that time is of no relevance to the spirit unless confined in the human world, where measurement is part of your perception, but for the sake of answering this question, I will assume that you know that I know what you mean.

There is a process which takes place between lives that has to happen in order for the new incarnation to take place. This process would occur in what you term the 'between-life' stage. I assume that when you refer in your question to time, you are asking in regards of human lifetime? To this I must say that there is no exact time between lives and no reason for one space between lives to others.

If I tell you there are incarnations that take place within a second of your time, while others have taken thousands of your years, it will give you more of an idea of how little is the importance of time when it comes to talking about the spirit world.

Even if we do not remember our previous, past or spirit life, will we remember it when we return to spirit?

Yes, but not in the human way of remembering. Memories to the human brain are like little messages which can be fleeting and short. They often appear as pictures which may invoke a feeling in you that even causes an emotion.

It is difficult for the human mind to hold on to a memory. To the spirit, thought is a living energy and therefore your spirit memory is more like an experience in insight. Each memory will be felt and understood in an instant and will enhance your very being.

The capacity to remember from all the lives you have lived is also available to you and you can, if allowed, assimilate the memories of others in the same way which you access your own. So, to put it in a slightly different way, you are your memories and they have much more importance to you because, in the spirit world, thought is as real as a physical experience is to you.

What is the purpose of living different lives?

I would have thought that it was quite clear to you by now that each life lived has an important element of growth and expansion for your consciousness. If there was no progression in conscious awareness, is it not true that the human being would not have evolved out of his most basic nature, which was much more ignorant and intuitive at best?

If you understand this, then maybe now you will see that each lesson learned is adding information to the mind and allowing it to desire expansion. It is this spiritual desire which causes the consciousness to continue to want to move forward, grow and develop in awareness.

It would be like a child born into this world with no desire to progress. Such a child would remain like a child and would constantly depend on its parents to feed it and fetch things for it. But, is it not that a child, when ready, wants to explore and grow? Its very desire to do this will make it move towards what it sees and want to touch and experience what feeling is, and so on.

Therefore, just like the small child, the young consciousness was driven by the same desire to experience all that was within reach, until other things came into view as its understanding grew. I hope this answer gives you a better understanding of spiritual growth through experience.

Do we have a choice not to come back into the physical life and, if we get tired of living as a human being, can we just stay in the spirit world?

You ask this question from a human perspective and as someone in the middle of that existence, but if you could be in your spirit body right now, the way you inquired would be very different indeed. Remember, from the spirit's point of view, there is no time.

So to be able just to experience that is quite something, but more than this, to have the opportunity to experience what it feels like to go through all the different changes one does as a human being is the greatest challenge of all.

But as the experience is so short, not all things can be accomplished in one life, so more and more becomes the desire of the spirit to experience life after life in the physical existence. There is a point, though, when the consciousness can enlighten itself to a state of luminosity, where it need not return to this realm and has experienced all things required to bring its consciousness to a state beyond any words I would have at my disposal.

Remember, children of the Earth plane, this state is open to all of you and all you have to do to achieve it is continue to grow and expand. Continue to refine your understanding and purify your consciousness with each experience within each journey you make.

Summary

When looking back over these questions and the answers that came through from the spirit world, I am reminded how sure my guides are of their answers, whereas people are often undecided or vague in their approach. It is always uplifting to hear this kind of certainty in spiritual matters. In my work as a medium I am very reassured because of this and the trust I already have for my spirit guides seems to double.

By its very nature, this particular subject seems to divide people's thoughts, especially in the matter of predestiny, where it poses the questions: 'Do we give ourselves difficult situations in our life, and if so, why?'

It is not in our human conditioning to think that we have planned to have a difficult life, yet according to Master Chi, that is exactly what we do. In one session when he came to speak to a group several years ago in London, someone asked if people with disabilities were being punished for things they had done in previous lives. His answer made everyone, including the questioner, look at the whole subject of disability and hardship in a very different way.

He began his answer by saying that no matter how deformed a human body was, we had to know that the spirit was always perfect. Then he continued to tell us that there are times when the consciousness decides to take on such hardship in the physical world, because it wants to burn up as much karma in one life as possible. So it creates such an obstacle for them to endure through the human life, as such a lifetime brings great enlightenment, much more than an average safe life.

Therefore we should look at people with disabilities with great respect, as they are truly brave, and sometimes we are to be pitied for choosing a safe life.

Since hearing this answer, I have certainly looked differently on anyone going through a hardship on their journey through life and it opens my own thinking of what is important in my own life. I find that I am less likely to judge others than I used to, and I have more of an understanding of my own difficulties and find it much easier to accept and learn from them. It also makes me look at my own karmic bank balance and wonder how much I am carrying in this life.

3

Karma and Rebirth

Introduction

I have met so many people on my journey who throw the word 'karma' about, yet do not seem to have any real understanding of what they are talking about when they use the word.

I know that when I was younger I thought karma was punishment and in some ways there is a come-back, more than a punishment, when we think of karma. But in the true meaning of the word, there can be the same return of good karma coming back to us when we practise good things.

I also had a difficult time when I was younger trying to figure out reincarnation and rebirth, when it was said that we live time and time again, and how we do so can relate to how we lived our life before.

In all the years I have studied both subjects and allowed my opinions and beliefs to change and grow, I can honestly say that I learned and understood so much more from the answers that came through from the spirit world on karma and rebirth than I did from any other means.

The answers which Chi and the other guides bring through seem to make sense and are quite uncomplicated.

What is karma and how does it work?

You ask about karma, this simply means actions; therefore, each action a person makes, or in some cases doesn't make, will make up their karmic balance. Also, you ask, how does it work? Well, there is such a lot to learn in a single lifetime before a person can truly understand the totality of karma in all levels, so let me give the first, most simple lesson, in karmic balance.

It is not so difficult to understand the fundamentals of karma when you first learn to take responsibility for the actions you make in life. The first thing being that for every action made, it will cause a reaction. So producing a negative action will result in a negative return to you at some point and a positive action will in the same way create a good return.

This is easy to control when you are master of all that you do and think, but for the student who naively believes he is a victim of higher forces, then it is time to begin a practice of self-awareness and learn from this first, most simple principle.

Can our karma affect our next life? For example, if we have bad karma, will we be in a worse life?

It is interesting that you ask this question so soon after the previous question. Take time to try and understand more the working of karma through the experiences of this life, but it is good that you concern yourself about what is to come, as it conditions the mind to create better actions in this lifetime.

All that you do in any lifetime is preparation for the next stage of living you move into. But what I say as guidance for you is that if you put more focus on creating good actions in this life, and taking responsibility for any previous bad or even mis-understood actions you may have made, then you need worry less about what is to come. Remember, it is the curse of ignorance that hides the light of truth from the student's eyes.

Can we go backwards with our karma even if we have been good in a previous life?

Yes, the responsibility of any life lies at the heart of self. This is why, when the consciousness becomes truly awakened, you must learn to be mindful; the higher part of the mind when awake will act like the parent to the lower self, who is like a child and is governed by need and will naturally often act out of necessity.

So it is important, when you have grown to a point of creating good deliberate actions that are appropriate, to be as ever watchful from the higher perspective, or by the law of karma your lower actions will bring about more difficult effects in your future life.

If we do bad things will that affect our spirit guide's karma for not being able to guide us correctly?

No, the mantle held by the spirit guide is that of one who oversees, and not one who controls. Therefore, his karma is neutral at all times.

The spirit guide is a manifestation of the student's mind until the student has progressed enough spiritually to realize true spiritual understanding of the contract between himself and the spirit guide.

The spirit guide is beyond emotion and therefore will not act out of need, keeping his energy clear of karmic reaction.

Do we have a choice of connecting to our loved ones again in future lives?

In some cases. To be in control of choosing where you are reborn in the physical world would mean that you had control of the consciousness before your bodily death, but there are groups of consciousness that travel together and will often return to the physical and spirit worlds together, if not in the same roles as they previously shared.

This is why you sometimes get the thought that you know a person who should feel more like a stranger to you. It is not uncommon that such groups are pulled together to share lessons many times. There is much more happening than I can share with you at this moment.

Do countries or nationalities have karma?

Indeed they do. Just like there are groups of people in this world whose journey is connected, there are areas that pull the travelling consciousness because of past actions and events; even times can be affected by karma, drawing certain pools of consciousness towards them.

This type of karmic pull is something I would like you to ponder on, but not get too involved and caught up in. Remember, there are some things your own mind can process and can even affect outcome, but this type of karma is above you for now, just know that it occurs.

Can we learn to control our karma and make a better life?

At some point on the journey of consciousness, it is your duty to take responsibility for all that you do and when that time comes you will change your karmic balance for the better. Just by thinking it and asking the question means that you have already begun, I'm glad to say.

Do animals reincarnate and do they have the chance to grow in the spirit world?

Animals are sentient beings; they have the same life-force running through them as you do. It can be seen throughout the animal kingdom that there are levels of intelligence and understanding as there are in the human world.

So, does this not tell you that they are capable of the same kind of spiritual evolution as humans? Remember, it is the consciousness that evolves, the body it takes on is but a manifestation of all of its former actions.

Can our guide choose to reincarnate and stop being a guide?

When we have grown to a point of enlightenment, all things are possible, but if you have made that contract, spiritually, then it would not be possible for such a thing to happen.

Is there ever a point when you wouldn't need to improve your karma?

The time when no actions are required is the time when you are no more. Even the quietest thought of self rings through existence and holds on to identity, but to be silent of self in all actions extinguishes all need and allows one not to be. This is when karma moves no more and stillness reigns.

Summary

Of all the subjects addressed in this book, karma and rebirth were asked about more than any other. Many of the questions asked were on a personal level, which makes it difficult to show them here because of their personal nature, and also because the answer often relates only to the person who has asked the question.

But there is one that I would like to share with the reader. It was asked during a trance session I gave in Germany not so long ago, by a young man who had never experienced sitting in a session with an entranced medium.

His question was about his two young children: they were twins, yet it seemed they were as opposite as twins could be. He wanted to know if they had joint karma; by this he meant that had they done something in a previous life, which brought them together in this one. He also wanted to know if one was good and the other was bad, because he said that their individual personalities reflected this.

Chi spoke to the man and everyone listened intently to what was coming through. He said that there is always a connection between multiple births in this world, but that both twins were individual consciousnesses, with individual paths in front of them. The fact that the father felt that one portrayed good actions, while the other bad, had no bearing on the past, but was more to do with the now.

He continued to inform the gentleman that the personality of both his twins would be the one thing that would highlight their individuality in this life and what he had perceived as good and bad was more to do with boldness and meekness.

The man agreed immediately and I think that everyone else got the picture of one dominant child and one very passive child, but the last part of the answer was what gave everyone a laugh.

Chi told the man that his wife was very dominant and that he was much less so in their relationship and he then asked if either child had a parent they clung to more. The man shared with the entire group that his wife did wear the trousers in their marriage and was the dominant one, and that his son, who seemed more bonded to his wife, was indeed the more dominant child over the daughter he thought was the good child.

The last part of Chi's message to him was this:

It is true what I said that your children will be distinguished through their own individual personalities, but please allow them to form that for themselves.

4

On Death and Dying

Introduction

On the question of death, I have my own understanding of what happens when the human life comes to a close and the spirit moves on to the other side. Although I must say that it has taken me many years and thousands of messages from the spirit world to form such an understanding.

I think back to when I was a small boy and had no real religious background. Neither of my parents lived by any religious code or practice and therefore I never had any thoughts of an after-life. God was only something I learned about in school; as an infant we were taught Bible stories and I remember it all felt very hard to take in.

The first time I can recall thinking about the after-life was after my grandfather died when I was ten years old and something inside of me just knew that he wasn't truly dead. This might sound like the wonderings of a child, but even then I had some awareness of his spirit around me from time to time. Shortly after this my cousin Steven, who was my age, died of cancer. Even though I felt more of a sadness about his passing, I still knew that his life-force had not gone forever.

I had so many occasions in my young life when spirits visited me; either in dreams or actual appearances, where they told me something that was about to happen, or in some cases things that had already happened but were at that moment unknown to my parents. It was this information, which always turned out to be true, that made me even more certain that the so-called dead were actually still in existence somewhere and that they had a better understanding of life than we did.

Since my early twenties I have been developing my gift of mediumship and through this practice I have had so many episodes in my life with the spirit world that I have formed more than a belief in the after-life. In fact, I would now say that I *know* it exists. More people have asked me questions about death and what it will be like when we first cross over than I can remember, but over the period of my adulthood my own view of what happens has changed, because of the different experiences I have had.

No matter how much it has altered, my one certain view of the after-life is that it is real and we will live on. However I feel that each individual will experience their own idea or perception of the spirit world in their own way, depending on how advanced their mind is at the point of crossing over. It has taken so much fear out of my life just to know that death is not the end of us; more than taking away my fear of dying, it has helped to take away my fear of living.

In this next chapter, my guides have given people the answers to their questions on this subject and once again I am surprised by some of the answers.

Do we travel through a tunnel when we die?

It would seem to the human mind that it is in a state of high-speed travel when it first leaves the body, but it is more to do with the quickening of vibration, which causes the sense of acceleration.

What you must understand is that the spirit body and the physical body vibrate at very different frequencies and unless you are practised in quickening your vibration, the transition from physical to spirit can produce a rushing sensation.

It will be different for different people and it will often depend on the death sequence. For instance, if the body has been going through the dying process slowly, the mind will have many opportunities to leave and come back; almost like a trial before the actual separation takes place.

In such circumstances the spirit body will adjust and there will be less sensation of travel. But in cases where the spirit body leaves the physical body abruptly, then there might be the sense of heightened speed and thrust.

No matter how the spirit leaves the body, there

will be a moment of light and serenity that will follow
and a state of grace will ensue thereafter.

Why have some people had experiences of near-death? Are they genuinely seeing the spirit world?

In many cases people get a glimpse of the spirit world
when they are near to physical death and, when they
do, they genuinely experience a moment in their spirit
body that allows them to see into the spirit world.
However, there are also those who do not reach the
heightened vibration required to open their spirit eyes,
and they experience nothingness for a moment and
sometimes darkness or blurred visions.

This would be like a baby who opens his eyes in
the human world for the first time; there is no proper
focus, and adjustment is required to see what is in
front of them. When the spirit comes into the spirit
world at the correct moment, there is always someone
there to take care of them and help them to adjust,
in the same way that the parents of the newborn
nurture it until it is settled into its new world.

Are there always spirit loved ones waiting to help us on the other side?

Indeed, for each spirit who returns to the spirit
world there is a welcoming party of a familiar spirit,
who will help to adjust the vibration of the returning

spirit until they are completely adjusted to their surroundings.

Also, the guide is always there and knows at exactly which moment they will return, so they are never alone. Even as you walk through your world you are never alone, your guide is always present in the spirit world watching over you, even if you do not know it.

How quickly do we adjust to the spirit world and what changes actually take place?

You ask this like it is a matter of time, but remember that there is no time in the spirit world and that it is more to do with the condition of the mind and the density of the light around the spirit body. If you consider it, some people take to change in their human life with great excitement, while others resist and distress about it.

In the spirit world there are those who come back ready and remember where they are, and excite and become bright almost instantly, but others need assistance.

By this I mean that the very presence of other spirits, who vibrate at a much higher pace, can bond with the new arrival and allow them to bask in their higher frequency until the realization of what has occurred to them is complete. At this moment the returning spirit will achieve harmony with the attending spirit and a new vision and clarity will fill their mind.

Do we still have a body of some kind when we leave the physical one behind?

Even now you have more bodies than you know. As the human body dies and the spirit body leaves, there are other bodily states to come through, which can also lead the consciousness to envisage a travelling sensation, but the travel that is actually taking place is through states of mind, or states of being.

Remember, you are coming from an existence where your body was your identity; therefore, it is still your greatest concept of identity when you reach the spirit world that you are in human form. So, if you understand that the mind created the idea of the physical body, then the mind can retain that same image until it no longer needs it, but the body would be more of a light-projected image of the physical body.

At this time, I will tell you, many of the ideas and creations which the human state of mind has created eventually dissolve and become light, in their version of what they were required to be when the body was in the physical world. Also, again, there is no time period to the process of lightening of any aspect of the spiritual mind in the spirit world; each will process as they need to.

Is there ever a time when we reincarnate immediately and not go into the spirit world?

No matter how rapid the process of the change from life to life will require, all consciousness must pass through a higher, more light vibration, or spirit world, in order for the change to take place. It is important for you to understand that between lives, the most recent incarnation on the Earth plane must be processed into the higher consciousness, which at all time resides in the light of the spirit world. Therefore, each moment of that life is recorded and added to the higher consciousness, before it can be clear to emit a new essence of itself into the physical world, to begin a new incarnation.

One life should not be attached to what it was before or there would be confusion and disorder in the new life forming. But I remind you again that there is no time in the spirit world, and what may seem to you like a tiniest fraction of time can be enough for a consciousness to react to its next incarnation, if the need to do so is relevant.

There are so many levels of incarnation, that to tell you more than you can accept at any one time would be to try to teach an infant a lesson on the mathematical workings of the entire universe.

Do some spirits get stuck between the two worlds? And if so, how would you find your way out of it?

No, the spirit does not get stuck between worlds, as you say. What you may be referring to is the breakdown of the life that has just been left behind.

The first thing you need to know is that the spirit returns to the spirit world. The physical body will leave behind a sense of atmosphere for those in the human world who were attached to it. The memories of that physical life remain with the grieving parties who were connected to it.

Then there is an emotional body that has created and felt an entire emotional life; in some ways, your emotional body almost has a life of its own and is often stuck where it died on the Earth plane. This leftover residue of that emotional life, if potent enough, can sometimes form a ghost body, which is no more than a compilation of the more concentrated emotions of its former life.

But do not mistake this phantom body as the spirit, for it is not. The ghostly body which is left behind is formed of human emotions and has no connection to the spirit body, which is now free of the physical world.

Are you healed instantly when you reach the spirit world or is there a time that must pass before you are back to normal?

The healing of the spirit body is more of an adjustment of perception than the type of healing you would consider for the physical body when it is out of sorts. Spirits who come to assist the returning spirit are in harmony with their surroundings and just by being close can help to attune the new arrival to the frequency at which they vibrate.

In some ways it would be like tuning a musical instrument to the correct pitch that will work in harmony with all the other instruments in the orchestra. If you think more of pitch and vibration, you will understand more about the healing of the spirit than with medical procedures.

Can we hold our loved one's spirit back by grieving too much and, if so, would they be stuck?

Grief is a very natural response to the loss of a loved one on the Earth plane and no, it will not hold the spirit back or cause them to be stuck in some in-between place or other. But grief, if not understood in a lifetime, can hold the human mind in an in-between state, as it will become fixed on a death which it is helpless to change and this feeling of helplessness can form deep depression in the emotional body of the grieving person.

When a person dies, whom you are bonded to by love in the physical world, it is normal to want to have more of that life and the love which you shared in the lifetime together, but from the higher, more spiritual perspective, it is the one test that may take you beyond the human thinking and raise your mind to the conception that the love you had has survived and lives on, even after the physical loss you have experienced.

To the spirit, death is a release from the confinements of the limited human life and though you might have formed bonds of love with others in that life, when you return to your natural spirit state, you will remember that all that you just experienced was something you chose before the human incarnation began.

And you will also know that you are not disconnected from the grieving person and that at some point you will be connected again in the spirit world, as you were before you both decided to embark on the journey into the human existence for experience.

You will also know that you can watch over your human loved ones and be there for them, to help them retune when they come over; and therefore you are comforted by the understanding that you are exactly where you should be, because you also realize that you know now that bonds of love can never be broken.

Does it help the spirit to adjust on the other side when we pray for them?

There is a twofold answer to this question. The first part is about the one who is sending the prayers and good will to the spirit person. In the very action of prayer you are lifting your mind to a higher state and in this ascended state you are closer to them than you know. This is why people very often feel better after they have sent a prayer out of their thinking mind, or from the very heart of their being through chosen words of good intention.

Think for a moment what you do when you ask a higher power, any higher power, to help a loved one who you feel is out of your reach.

The first thing you do is to put that spirit person in the hands of that higher power and trust that they can help. Such actions or thoughts help to heal the one who is praying and caring, because it is an act of compassion which only serves to aid all concerned.

So good work is being done, whether you know it or not, yet something inside you will inform you that it is doing good. Again I say something, because even if you do not know what you are doing, you are in actual fact looking for healing on a higher level within yourself.

Now, the second part of this question that has to be answered is for the spirit loved one now in the spirit world. They will instantly feel your prayer and instantly know all that I have just told you, as it is the way of spirit to feel and understand. Therefore, if you are beginning any kind of healing process, it will lighten and brighten the spirit and, such as allow them to grow on the other side.

So remember this, it is a good thing for the human mind to enter into a prayer life when it comes to their loved ones in the spirit world, as all concerned can benefit from it.

Summary

There have been so many questions put to my spirit guide over the years on the subject of death; so many were personal and meant something only to the person who put the question to Chi. However I feel that it would be wise to share a couple of these with you as there may be a more universal answer within them, which might help others in similar positions.

The first question that comes to my mind is when a woman in her late forties asked Chi about her son, who had recently passed away. She wanted to know who was with him and if he was at peace.

Chi stood my body up from the sitting position and walked me towards the lady, then he extended my hand in a gesture to the woman to stand and put her hand in mine. The group who were present at this trance session went very silent and the fascination as to what was about to happen could be felt around the large room we were in.

He told the woman that her son was at peace and that he was sorry for his action; by this he meant his suicide, which had not actually been mentioned at this point. He went on to give a description of how the young man was feeling near the end of his physical life and what drove him to commit such an act. It was at this point that Chi gave the name of the lady's father and said that he had come to fetch his grandson at the very moment his life ended in this world.

He also told the lady that this was the information she had come for and that there was another person in the group whose family were suffering in the same way and this was why the message he brought forward was important: so that both families might take some solace from it. At the end of this session, I believe that the entire group took something from Chi's words.

The other message I felt was important was for a father, who asked my guide if his son was cold beneath the ground and could he please give him some evidence to say that he wasn't. Chi told the man that his son was not beneath the ground anymore and that his spirit in its new form was anything but cold.

But he almost reprimanded the gentleman, telling him that he should stop sleeping on his son's grave, that he had other family who needed him, and that his spirit son was concerned for his wellbeing and indeed his life.

When I came out of the trance the man spoke to me, asking me how this entity knew that he was sleeping over his boy's grave. All I could do was assure him that I could not possibly have prior knowledge of such a thing and that the information he received could only have truly come from one source: his son in the spirit world.

I do believe that such accounts are important to share with others, especially when people are so grief stricken that they cannot move forward in their own life because of the loss of a loved one.

Also, it is important to point out that Chi sometimes gives evidence to people during trance sessions that completely changes their views on death and dying, and I can assure you that I have no idea how any trance session will go before it starts, nor do I even know if it will happen, because there are occasions when the spirit chooses not to come.

5

Phenomena and Paranormal Activity

Introduction

There are so many things between heaven and earth
that we do not know about, as well as some on earth
itself. I have spent a life trying to understand some
of the strange happenings that have occurred in both
my own life and the lives of many people who have
come to me to try and find solutions.

I suppose that my mind seems to accept that I
won't be able to answer all things in this life, but
they happen to make me think and I would assume
that this is the case for others, too.

As people, we still have much to learn about the
complexities of our own human mind, not to mention
our spirit and what that entails. There are some things
I am certain we are not meant to have the answers
to in this life and therefore they must remain in the
box marked unexplained, but other strange and paranormal things happen to show us a new way, or to
broaden our mind.

I have found that when we can see phenomenal
things without fear in our hearts, we are so much

closer to understanding them, and maybe even learning to bring about incredible changes to our lives and the lives of others.

Too many people throughout history have seen, heard and felt bizarre things that are not supposed to happen, for it all to be just coincidence or delusion. There are so many people since man has been on this planet who have displayed gifts that defy logic and in many cases physics. In this section I love to read back the answers that my guide has given, because to the spirit world, nothing is phenomenal; they seem to accept that all things are possible.

Why do some people have gifts or abilities to cause phenomena in mediumship or healing?

Just as some people have the aptitude for music, art, science or poetry, there are those who are born with a more attuned sensitivity and awareness of states of life that others cannot even imagine for one moment. The same would be said for those who are natural healers and come to this world to make people feel better, because they bring with them a heightened and awakened sense of compassion with them.

But, young one, let me assure you that every human being possesses a gift of the spirit or higher consciousness, if they truly look for it during their life. Is it not so that some people only discover their gifts at the end of their human existence?

Then understand this, the gift that was recognised much later was always there, and only through certain circumstances and experiences was it allowed to surface. So I say to you, young one, have you discovered your true spiritual gift in this lifetime?

No, not yet, but I am still looking.

I know and I am allowed to tell you that you are looking in the right place, but don't forget to look at what is right in front of your face, for very often you set your sights too far in the distance and miss what is right in front of you.

Is a poltergeist a bad spirit and why would this energy be allowed to cause people to be frightened?

The term you have used, poltergeist, does this not relate to a noisy ghost? If it does, then at once we have cleared the thought that it is Spirit in any form. The ghost, or leftover emotional body, or even stain from the distressed human life, is what will form a ghost, but the noisy ghost you ask about does not even come from this source.

No, the energy that causes the disturbance associated with the poltergeist is to do with the unsettled human who is holding, deep within them, the fear and angst which is not being recognized by those around them, even in cases where someone close to them has left their life.

The built-up frustration, anger, jealousy or maybe even hatred is what causes such phenomena. Sadly for you, you cannot see anger when it is cold and sits deep within another person. Not only is it cold, but it becomes menacing and malevolent; at this stage, it can become explosive.

Do not mistake human rage for anger, they are very different emotions and it is the first I spoke of, the cold stifled anger that is capable of escaping and becoming more concentrated and physical at some point.

Let me put it to you like this: if you believe that there is a force within the human consciousness that can love and heal and help by love, then that same human consciousness can hate and destroy and damage. Remember, I said human consciousness and not eternal spirit.

Is it possible to see into the future?

There are times when you may be able to see into the future, but there are different ways in which future events can be seen. The first thing you should note is that the future in the human world is always in a state of change and therefore only when there is certainty that one event will follow another can an opening in time appear.

If you try to predict an outcome of something

which isn't certain, then the vision you seek will not appear, or in fact may appear as a convoluted selection of events in chaotic fashion, which will seem to have no meaning whatsoever.

More often than not, when a person gets a glimpse of something in the future, it is random rather than deliberate. This type of vision may occur when the person is in a dream state. When you are in such a state your mind is between worlds, the world of the spirit, as your spirit returns there when the body sleeps, and the physical world which you are returning to.

In the spirit world there is no time whatsoever, and in a state of no time, one can look in all directions of time, past, present and future. So when the consciousness is returning to the human state, it may remember a glimpse of the future.

There have been in past times, and indeed even today, people in your world who could induce an altered state of mind that would allow them to look into the future and return to the human consciousness with information of things to come, but again, their mind was in an in-between state, where time is relevant and not.

This would be a good time for me to speak to you about time itself. In the briefest way possible, I will try to explain how time and events which take place within it look from the spirit perspective.

From the moment you come into this world you are on a particular line of time which will go forward from the second you decide to take human form. During the lifetime, you will have choices to make; each choice you make will determine what timeline your life will follow.

You may decide to choose one thing over another in your life which will cause you to change direction. In the same way that a train can move from one track to another, diverting its course to another place, your important decisions during your life's journey may alter your line of time and the future events and experiences in your life.

If you remember, this is why I said earlier that the future in the human world is uncertain. There is much more to talk about within this subject, but I feel that at this point you have had more than enough to digest.

Can spirits materialize in this world and if so, how do they do that?

Yes is the simple answer to the first part of your question. On the second part, where you ask me how can they do this, then I will try to be as clear as possible, because you are asking me to describe something from a metaphysical viewpoint and make it understandable in the human sense.

The first thing you should look at is that all life is energy and vibrates at a relevant rate to its reality. So, if a spirit vibration was one million vibrations per second of your time, then no device in the human world could measure it, but it is there. None of your senses are equipped to pick up such a form of energy, but because you cannot detect it in your world doesn't mean that it is not there.

Now, if the spirit needed to come into the human world to appear as a vision of their former self, then they would have to find a way of slowing down their vibration and projecting an image of themselves, using what you would term as 'telepathy'.

Also, they would require the use of energy more dense than the spirit, so from the atmosphere they would use some of the particles to form a denser energy around them, like a cloak. This is why it has been said many times by people who have experienced a vision of a materialized spirit that the air around them turned cold; they felt cold as the particles of heat were drawn together around the forming image. And elements of the witness, or witnesses, may also be used to build a force dense enough to mould into a likeness of the spirit's former human identity.

This type of practice can leave people feeling drained and exhausted if not correctly managed. In the cases of mediums who allowed themselves to be used for such a practice, the entranced medium would feel effects of tiredness and lightheadedness at the end of their session, because their own body chemicals would have been used by the spirit control in order to create the linking of the two worlds.

There would also be an element of dehydration happening around the body, as body fluids would also be used to build the energy which acts as a substance to allow the spirit to form in a recognizable image.

There are many reasons why Spirit choose not to use this type of mediumship now, but that is for a different question on a different day. So in order for the two worlds to meet, energies have to be used from the atmosphere and humans, and vibration must be slowed down. This is the simple answer, but I assure you, it is much more involved than that.

If spirits are so evolved and good, why are people so frightened by the thought of seeing one?

This is a very good question, my young friend, but one which does not have an easy answer. I say this to you because people vary so much in their individuality. Therefore it is difficult to say one thing for all people. Even as you ask the question, I can sense that there are some among you who would love to witness a vision of a spirit person, is this not so?

Several people responded 'Yes!' at the same time.

So, for you people who desire such a phenomenon, there is in fact no need for an answer, because you are at a point when fear of spirit no longer fills your mind. But for those who do have fear, and as long as there is even one who would be afraid of this type of occurrence, I can assure you that it will never happen.

Remember, it is not the wish of the spirit world to scare people; no, our wish is to enlighten the human mind and guide them to solutions in their life, which will have the effect of helping them to overcome their fears. Something makes me want to say to you at this moment that maybe it is not a spiritual vision that brings fear, but a reminder of death, and its uncertainty for the human mind is what is truly frightening if such a situation should occur.

Why do so many paranormal things happen in the early hours of the morning? Is there a time when spirits can enter our world more easily?

There is some truth in your question that it might be easier at a certain time for the spirit to come into your world, but it is more to do with you, and the fact you are in a much more spiritual state at this time, that you may see the spirit world or a spirit person. It is maybe not so clear to you that spirits are always close to you, but you have not the capacity to sense us.

When your mind is shutting down from this world due to tiredness, you are actually entering an in-between state, so now think of what I have said and visit the possibility that it could be you appearing to the spirit, rather than the spirit appearing to you.

Can you imagine the fright the spirit person would get to see a human appear out of nowhere?

Many people laughed at this point, as they all understood, in that moment, that my guide had a sense of humour and was jesting with them.

Even after death we keep our sense of humour, my friends. So if we also then can see when you are in a more subtle state of mind such as sleep, or even going into sleep, and also there can be a point as you come out of your sleep when the two worlds are closer, phenomena are more likely to happen. You only have to look at the time of the day or night when most people return to the spirit world at the end of their human life; you will find that it would be in, as you called it, the early hours of the morning.

There are other things that could be said about the conditions which are created by the stillness of this time, and also the atmosphere in the human world around this time of day is very different to the more waking hours of a daytime, but as regards this question, I feel that you have had enough for now.

Are there life forms on other planets in the universe?

Of course there are other forms of life in the universe. It would be very wrong of you to assume that in a universe with such a vast scale, which is filled with life-giving elements and components, that life would evolve from just one planet.

Remember, the very planet you live on is alive and it is the planet that sustains you with all of the life-giving elements it provides, but am I to assume that your question was geared more to the existence of advanced beings that travel on vehicles which travel at light speeds and beyond?

Yes, Chi, that is what I meant. I am sure you are correct in saying that there are other forms of life out there, probably in all shapes and sizes, but I would like to know more about extraterrestrials. If you know what I mean?

Young man, I feel certain that you do not even know what you mean, but I will endeavour to describe what I know of such life forms. There is a reason that you are only allowed to know certain things while going through your human existence. Try to think for one moment how advanced a species would have to be in order to travel around galaxies and the universe. If a species has ascended to such risen minds, full of knowledge and technical capabilities, then it would also have grown beyond much of the restricted thinking that confines the human mind; to evolve to such an extent would bring with it spiritual evolution, also.

What I am trying to say is that such an evolved

species would know not to upset the balance of the Earth and all the life she sustains, so think of the evolved ones more like guardians and onlookers; your big brother, if you like.

If there are other life forms in all parts of the universe, does each one have its own after-life?

All of life which has a beginning and end returns to the same spirit world. You must remember, death affects only the physical life. I say this because it is only the limited physical life forms that will experience a death.

The spirit, or subtle life-force, was there before, during and after the human episode. The same would apply to any other life which has manifested in a dense form for a period of time. Remember, that which comes into time will at some point go out of it.

When thinking of the spirit world, try not to attach boundaries or limitations. The existence out of time is boundless and, in your present state, you will not be able to fathom such, but always strive to stretch your boundaries, which are part of your journey back to enlightenment. I must also take this moment to congratulate you on the question you chose to put to me. I have never been asked this question before, so thank you, young one.

The miracles described in the Bible, did they actually occur and, if so, how can they be done?

Such phenomena are not impossible when you have an expanded consciousness. In the physical world there have been many miracles; such displays of the power of nature, if and when they do occur, are not to bring one person superiority over other men.

No, they are done to draw attention to something much greater and that is the truly spiritual force behind them. For nature to be bent in such a way would have brought with it attention beyond anything which could have been imagined, back in the time on Earth when this was supposed to have taken place. So ask yourself, did it?

Also, ask yourself if there was an after-effect that lasted way beyond the so-called miracles themselves, and if you think there was, then maybe that's because such profound episodes would, by their very nature, leave traces and remnants that would travel on in time long after they took place. Are people still talking about them?

On any question of belief, I offer it to you to make your own decisions; it is not my course to make you believe in something or not. I can give guidance and answer questions, but not control or manipulate your thinking. So, just know that nature can be bent by one who has mastered their own conscious mind and who has understanding of the very workings of nature, but why they would do so would only be to teach that all is not quite what it seems in the material world.

Can we learn to develop some of these gifts? And what is the best way to do this?

I would remind anyone who wishes to develop the ability to use gifts of a higher nature to try first to develop your own awareness of self. Many people are born into your world with gifts of a super- and paranormal nature.

Some do not wish to use them, nor develop them further; this, of course, is their choice to do so or not. Others display their heightened abilities to gain notoriety and fame and to stand out and be noticed, liked, and even loved and adored by others.

The gift is not the key ingredient here. It is the one who uses the gift who needs to develop in order to use it properly, with both compassion and wisdom. If you wish to embark on a long journey which will involve discovering self, that means the good and bad, the right and wrong of one's life, then yes. You should go forward and develop yourself and the gifts of the spirit will develop with you. Remember, a gift without compassion is merely a trick and when wisdom is absent, then the gifted one is still a novice in his craft.

To all of you, I say this. When it comes to spiritual gifts, do not be in a rush to obtain them. No, it is better that you work on the person who will one day be worthy of using such life-changing commodities.

Summary

Phenomena and paranormal questions are always asked of my guide when he comes through in these trance sessions. In my own life, I have experienced so much phenomena that my whole understanding of the nature of things in this world has truly shifted. But when I think of all the things I've seen, heard and experienced, there is one which stands out above the others, and it is this.

I was somewhere in my middle-twenties at the time and I was only in the early stages of my development when this took place. In the street where I lived, there was a very sad and tragic happening, when a woman – who lived directly across the road from me – was killed by a car as she was walking across the street. It was one of those terrible occurrences that, as you can imagine, shook the entire neighbourhood.

The strange event that totally blew my mind took place on the day after this lady's funeral. She had left behind her husband and two young children who were around the ages of seven and nine. I was quite shocked when there was a knock on my door and, as I opened it, both the children were standing in front of me, demanding that I went to see their father as quickly as possible.

Without thinking, I followed the children as they ran back towards their house. I entered the open door to find not only their father, but two other neighbours, gathered in the living room at the end of a small hall. I was about to ask what was so urgent, when the father told everyone to be silent and to listen; he said it was about to happen again. I was not the only one looking bewildered.

The six of us were all standing in a small living room, which measured about twenty square feet. In the room there was a sofa and two armchairs, a television set, display cabinet, coffee table and other items of furniture. Then from absolutely nowhere there came a gentle rapping sound and, as if by magic, a very powerful force, like a warm wind, blew through the room.

The carpet then lifted two to three feet into the air and swayed like a wave upon the sea, rising and falling, and although we all felt as if we were raised up with it, none of us seemed to move. You would think that this would have alarmed us, but no, everyone felt an overwhelming feeling of joy as this powerful force moved around us, under us and through us, all at the same time. When the phenomenon stopped, all the adults walked to the edges of the carpet to examine it and we found that it was still nailed tightly to the floor.

Everyone looked at me for an answer, for even though I was not known as a medium at that time, many of my neighbours knew that I attended the spiritualist church; indeed, that is why I'd been sent for, in the hope that I could bring answers.

One of the people asked quite simply, 'What just happened?' The children were laughing and everyone else had at least a smile on their face. Something inside me told me that it was their mother and I tuned in my mind without saying anything to anyone.

I felt the lady's presence at once and I got a message for her husband and children, which I did not want to speak out in front of the others who were there at that time. Remember, I was still very much in the development stages of my mediumship.

The phenomenon repeated itself several times, before the neighbours left and I had a chance to talk with the family. I told them that I felt that it was the lady trying to let them know she was with them, and the fact that her force made everyone happy, including her children, meant she was at peace. The moment I began to give the message the phenomenon ceased, never to happen again.

Some years later I was in my home circle and, as I would be in trance, I asked one of the other sitters to ask my guide Master Chi about this incident; I wanted to hear what the spirit world had to say about such phenomena. Chi came through and my friend put the question to him. His answer was so simple and, I am sure, perfectly correct. He said:

What is so phenomenal about a mother wanting to come back to her loved ones? Why would she

not wish to make her children feel her presence
and make them feel happy and safe? The force
which Gordon described that he felt was quite
simply a mother's love. When love is involved
anything can be moved.

I wanted to share this account with you, because
so many people think that whenever there are
phenomena, they are negative; in my experience, this
is simply not so.

6

Guides, Angels and Ascended Masters

Introduction

I meet more and more people on my travels, working as a medium, that want to know if they have a spirit guide, or an angel of some kind, who guides them from above.

There seems to be a whole new wave of people who are open to the idea of having a connection to the higher world and, as well as the numerous books and teachings there are on such subjects, many of them want to have their own personal spiritual teacher to lead them on their journey.

It is all very well, and even romantic, to think of having a guide, or angel, for yourself, but you must remember that the connection to higher spiritual beings does not happen so easily.

I have been developing through meditation exercises for over twenty-six years now and even though I have forged that link between the two worlds, it did not happen overnight. No, many things in my mind and my life had to shift and change before I could make such a contact and, even more than that, before I could begin to understand the connection to my spirit guide.

I do believe that many who inquire about the ascended teachers see such matters as all in the mind and that is okay. But, for those who are serious about making a deeper link to their guide and wanting to raise their spiritual vibration in order to do so, then more dedication is needed.

It is inevitable when I am giving a trance session and my guide Chi comes through, that people will ask questions of him about ascended masters, guides and angels. In many cases they feel satisfied with the answers they have received, but sometimes Chi's direct words can change a person's perspective of the whole subject and shift the foundations of what they first thought. In this next session, many minds were changed.

Is there such a thing as an angel and if so, how would you describe it?

When you say an angel, I assume you are referring to a tall human-like creature dressed in white, who has wings attached to his back and descends from the heavens, bathed in a celestial light. Is this not so?

Yes, it is.

Then let me explain that this image was first brought to the world through the spoken word and was therefore a description given by one man to another. His description was his interpretation of what he experienced during a spiritual experience with a high spiritual being, that bore a message for him from the higher world.

Now, the listener who was moved by this account formed his own image of the being, and so described it to others when repeating the story told to him by the first man, and so on and so forth. The moment that this image came into your world through the medium of painting it became a standard and accepted concept of what a higher, more spiritual light-being should look like.

But let me tell you that other descriptions of light-beings have been given throughout the journey of mankind, but have never been drawn or painted, because they were formless and the teller of the story could not find words to describe them in any known form.

The overwhelming power of the light-being left the recipient of the experience without words, but in essence the two experiences could be called visitation of the angels to this world.

Also, remember the word or name 'angel' is of human origin, as there are no words for such a highly evolved pure being; so already man has created the angel in his own way in order to make sense of it.

The second part of your question was how I would describe an angel. Well, I wouldn't try. To try to put a description onto that which is clear would only serve to lessen its purity; but do remember, there have been men who have seen a highly evolved spiritual being, a spirit guide, and described it as an angel from heaven, so you must understand that when the human mind has any spiritual visitation, the truth of what has occurred may be lost and humanized in the translation from experience into words.

So I know that there are levels of spirit so pure and beyond my own comprehension and therefore until I have risen in vibration they shall remain such.

There are so many ways to answer this question, but I will leave it at this point, because you must try to take in what I have said. When you understand the answer I have given to you just now, then you may be ready to see it from an even higher point of view, but remember, young one, take one step at a time; do not try to understand the heavens, when you haven't yet understood you.

Does everybody have a spirit guide?

Yes, I could just give you this as an answer, but I really think you want me to elaborate more. All of life is guided by a higher force, a more spiritual force that runs parallel with their earthly journey.

Many people will never make this connection in their physical lifetime, but nonetheless the guide will not leave them but instead take note of the life and the choices they make in that life.

You see, part of being the guide is also to monitor the decisions and actions the person carries out in their human life; to note how many lessons are truly being learned. Our job is not to stand by and wait until you call on us to help you. No, sometimes you miss the picture of what the role is of the spirit guide.

Much like the idea of the angel, the guide is a mediator between heaven and earth, the spirit world and the human world. Much of what happens in your world has an effect on the higher world, so the guide is there as much to protect the higher world from the effects of the lower world.

There now, I bet you wish I had stuck with the first yes.

Do we have more than one guide?

In actual fact, the human mind can create all sorts of manifestations when thinking about the spirit world and let me tell you that the spirit will always accommodate you if there is a positive reason you need to adopt such an idea. But remember, we see things from a higher perspective and know the truth.

If your child is happy with just one toy, then that is a contented child, but if he needs to have more than one, you may feel he is a needy child. If that same child has more than one toy but plays with them to create situations that satisfy him, then it was a worthwhile thing to give him the second toy, because he has increased his satisfaction and brought even more contentment to his mind.

The spirit guide in this case is like the parent and must make decisions as to what will help and hinder the progress of the child. So, in essence, what I am saying to you is that some of you will be given experiences with different spiritual beings, because it will further your knowledge and emotional intelligence; others might go off and confuse themselves with notions of many guides and spiritual beings surrounding them, but you only need listen to how that person is affected by such a thing. Are they grounded and rational about their spiritual journey? Or are they ungrounded and inappropriate in their conversations about their spiritual life?

In truth, you have one guide and one guide only. If your mind is truly opened then the guide may invite other spiritual teachers to you for further growth, but all the while there is only one guide.

Is it possible to have an angel as your spirit guide, or even have both?

Once again, my young friend, the very fact that you have asked such a question tells me that you have a need to own your spiritual beings and not try to understand their worth on your journey.

To you I would say, try to train more in self-awareness and truly get to know you before trying to understand the order of the higher worlds.

Previously I said that the spirit world will accommodate what you need and will adjust as long as it is productive to your progression, but if your mind becomes confused at the idea of having guides, angels, and all things shining, then we will step back and allow you to become more grounded in one reality.

I feel that this answer is more universal and all should take note of what has just been said. It is much better for you, as you try to open your mind and understand the spirit world around you, that you always, and as often as possible, have reality checks.

It is one thing to talk of guides and angels, but to know as much about yourself first is far more important. Whether you know it or not, whether you ever learn it in your lifetime on the Earth, the spirit world are watching over you and you will always be in our sight. It is good that you reach out to your higher spiritual nature and bring more spirituality into your world, but do not be in a rush to know everything at one time, or ask questions that even the cleverest answer you will not understand.

I say this to all of you, in order that you try to be slow and deliberate in your progression, learn to understand one thing before you seek to find answers to another. I may have given you what seems like a lecture in this answer, but I do so out of compassion for you, as any good parent would rather reprimand his child than see them hurt themselves unnecessarily.

Have we known our guide before this life or maybe even shared a life together before?

The bond between spirits is complete and when you ask about knowing, then it is so that you have known each other, but it is a much deeper knowing than the one you speak of. For you, knowing is more like encountering, or meeting someone. The fact is, in spiritual terms between the spirit in the spirit world and the human spirit, the term knowing is more like remembering.

If you think that when you are born into your new family, you don't know them, neither they you. But there is a familiarity, which grows as you grow as a sentient being, a remembering that opens the way to reaffirming the bond between you, which allows love to be felt, and it is love that re-ignites the connection that was always there, it was only asleep for a while.

Your relationship with your guide is the same, when you first enter the human world you are unable to remember anything of where you have come from, or why you are there. As your mind grows through your human life, some of you will get a calling, as it were, a sensation that you are disconnected from something or someone; this is your inner spirit looking for its connection to where it instinctively knows it is connected.

Sometimes during the human life, certain people experience the opening of the higher mind, and memories of where they have lived before come flooding into their consciousness from a time before, when they walked the Earth as someone else. Others may experience trips back and forward to the spirit world and touch the light they came from.

Such awakenings are not common, but do have meaning to those who receive them. Remember, when we think of Spirit, we think of interconnectedness and oneness, so we actually all know each other on some level, but let us leave that to another session, as it will take us in another direction.

Can a family member, or a beloved friend or partner, be your guide when they go to the spirit world?

No, the contract is already created before you are born and therefore the connections you make in the human life follow after this. But your loved ones, when they pass back to the spirit world, will always be able to watch over your life if they wish, and they will work with your spirit guide when they need to make you aware of their presence.

It is always difficult to be clear to you, when we talk about your loved ones on the other side, that they have expanded beyond the human that you knew and become their higher spiritual self, and have not the same attachment as you do.

By this I mean that they will be bonded to you always, because of the love that was shared and connected between you, but it is only the human emotions that cling to a relationship, either between loved ones, or indeed spirit guides, but my young friends, I do not expect you to fully understand the ways of Spirit at this point; the fact that you wish to does you all justice.

Are there guides above and guides like ascending masters?

Once again you categorize the spirit world. It is understandable because the human mind needs to work by levels and limitations, it has to develop an order by which it understands and this is fine to do, because it will not actually affect the boundless-ness of the spirit world, but when talking to other people you might upset their thinking if it is different from yours.

Let me try for a moment to make something clearer for you when it comes to the notion of higher spiritual teachers. The human mind works well when it thinks it is governed by authority and rank, class and status, but the same is not so for the higher consciousness.

The spiritual part of each of you will understand this in due course, as it is the way of enlightenment to become less important and trust to the way of things.

Could our spirit guide be part of our own higher consciousness?

This is a very good question and I am pleased that you have put this forward. To even consider that you are, in fact, two levels of consciousness running at the same time, through a human existence and co-existing in the spirit world, is the first step to your higher understanding of self.

This question shows me that you are less afraid than most people to accept that your individuality in the human world is not all that you are. No, you are a spirit being and part of you does exist in this very moment in two worlds.

As you would look at a ship on the ocean, you would only see what is visible to your eyes, but beneath the water there is an integral part of that vessel that keeps it afloat and allows it to travel through the water.

So it is the same with your consciousness. Part of you has manifested in a world where you can be seen, but another part of you is unseen, but very purposeful to the journey you are on.

It is so that as a human being you feel your individuality and this is as it should be, even though most of your human nature is a reflection of your spiritual self, which by its very nature wants you to connect through love.

In contrast to this, the higher part of your consciousness which exists in the spirit world is interconnected to all life, therefore you are me and I am you, as it were. Only the mind which is open will understand what I say right now and again I say, that is as it should be. For those who find this hard to comprehend, I say, leave it as such until your mind reaches out for such understanding.

The existence of consciousness is whole and one, therefore everything that is in existence is part of the same thing; only understanding, or the lack of it, can fracture this concept and break it down, causing confusion and in some ways disorder. But remember, young ones, everything in the universe is exactly where it should be in relation to the now.

Can our guides and angels still evolve and grow in the spirit world?

Yes, is the simple answer to your question, but once again I detect that more information of how is required.

All of life, no matter how ascended, must continue to grow and expand. This is the very nature of life. Just as the vast universe itself is in constant motion, always moving forward, and expanding in all directions at the same time, then do all things connected with it, spiritual, or ethereal. Again, I bring you back to the progression of knowledge in your world and how it is in constant motion to improve itself. In this example, you will recognize growth in a way you can understand it.

In much the same way, the spirit world is expanding and progressing, always refining and purifying, as is its nature to do so. Therefore, does it not become apparent to you that it is Spirit who refine and then there is an effect in your world and the human mind uplifts and more clarity comes into your world.

What I speak of will take thousands of your years to accomplish at a time, so do not be in a rush to see your world become enlightened in one movement of new life on the Earth. Although I spoke to you using time as the measurement of change in clearing the mind of man, I must say that it is more to do with motion than time, and by motion, again I do not refer to this in a physical way, but more of a natural surge of power in the universe itself.

So, to recap, as the spirit world refines and grows, which is always occurring, so too does the human world and any other world affected by this in the universe.

What is the best way to get to know your spirit guides?

The best way to get to know your spirit guide is first to get to know you. You are part of the same journey. You are made up of the same components, as it were, albeit spiritual elements. So when you learn to see yourself on a deeper level, you will be truly ready to open and accept that there is a higher part of you that is connected to another spirit, and so on.

As a practice, you should learn to feel the world around you and understand the effects of your feelings, and your senses, over your emotions. Use the five senses you have at your disposal to give you a perspective of the physical world you are a part of and learn what it means to be you in that state.

Be clear and truthful with yourself when it comes to your actions and your thoughts. When you have reached a point when you can control, from a higher perspective, how you act and think, then you are taking control of your life.

When you even show the first steps to doing this, the spirit guide will start to become much more apparent to you and his presence will be felt in your life. Remember, when the guide appears, or is sensed by you, you have given them permission to point you towards the plan you made before you came here. The guide has a much clearer understanding and vision of your plan and though he cannot make you do things, is always there to lead you to your lessons, and always there after each progression or failure you make.

Try in your eagerness to link with us, not to imagine us, but let us become a part of your reality; for as much as you can, let us into that reality, it is as strong as the bond between us will become during your walk through the human journey.

Summary

There is something so reassuring about knowing that you always have someone above you to guide, and on occasion advise you on your life's journey.

I remind so many people on this path that I do not always consult my guide, and that I prefer to make my own choices as much as I can, and even when that means making a mistake, I am willing to do that in order to truly feel the experience, as I believe that that is why we are in this world.

Although I have a contact with Chi, and I know he is always close to me, I try to be grounded as he has taught me so many times, and to really be a part of my physical life and existence. So many people I meet become overbearing when it comes to having spirit guides and angels in their lives and they tend to forget they are in this human world to experience physical and emotional lessons.

We must all remember to have a life while we are here and have a good spiritual contact, but remember to switch off as well. I do know people who do nothing but talk about the angelic worlds and their spirit guides, of which they say they have so many, and they seem to have such a need to live in that type of thinking. I do not think that type of thinking is healthy, that it becomes delusional and is not nurturing to you or your progression in this life.

I really do take seriously what Chi says in the last question he answered and I try to work on me, more than think about spiritual things. Even now when I do teachings about Spirit, I always advise people to work more on themselves for as long as they can, before even sending out that thought to spirit guides and so on.

To all who read this, I ask you to take your time and enjoy each lesson. This can be a wonderful life, full of magical experiences and happenings, but do not invent them for the sake of achieving things in a hurry. Let your experiences be deep, meaningful and true.

7
Religious Beliefs and Faiths

Introduction

I have never found myself to be very religious in my life, even though I have been fascinated by religions and their practices through the ages. I often get asked which religion I would follow should I want to and the only answer I have is Buddhism, simply because it is non-violent and deals a lot with the practice of compassion.

I do have great trust in my spirit guide Chi and the other guides. As far as I can remember, I have never heard anything about his own practice of religion, if he had one. By all accounts he appears to have had some connection to Taoism, but when asked, he only comes back with a clever answer that makes him sound disconnected from any religion known to man.

On a spiritual journey many people find religion, while others might lose theirs because of a new teaching that they pick up along the way, but as far as I can make out, religion still plays a big part of man's spiritual journey and it will for some time to come. I have never felt like preaching, or trying to convert people to my beliefs or understandings. It has always been my thinking that people should find their own path, even if that means that they have to walk many different ones before they decide which is right for them.

In this next session there are questions put to Master Chi about religion and I still find it very interesting to read how he answers each question with precision and without bias to one religion or another, and how he sees the spiritual practice as something much more useful to our growth than the religious one.

Is there a God or higher power that created life in this world and the universe?

There is most certainly a higher power that is responsible for all of creation. When you speak of God it sounds like an individual and that by its nature would be the very opposite of the creative force, but I understand exactly what you mean and why you would use this term.

If you could try to expand your understanding of the unlimited nature of what you call God, you would probably find a less limiting term to describe this force.

I say this to all of you at this time, that you must try to open your mind when thinking of the higher power in the universe. By opening your mind to the unlimited, you are embracing the spiritual part of yourself, and only then can you have even a fraction of the mind you would need to understand the higher creative forces and their direction and purpose. But, for now, try to expand yourself and the answer to this question will change.

Which faith is the best one to choose when it comes to religion? Is there one that is more true than the others?

Faith is not a religion; it is a form of trust, or belief in something which may never be proved. Religion is the creation of the human mind and may work for those who choose to put their faith in it. If you are asking me what will bring more spiritual enlightenment to your life, this is a very different matter.

The mind which is ready to grow will do so because it is ready. Such a mind will indeed grow through a religious practice, if it stays true to the pure principles of that doctrine and eventually reaches the highest point of clarity a human mind can achieve. The same mind will also expand the same way and achieve the same opened state by understanding its own experiences in life without a religious doctrine as a guide. So enlightenment will come when the consciousness is ready to expand anyway.

Like all things in the human world, religion has highs and lows, good and bad. Why is this, I hear you think. It is so because the human world is not perfect and even if the most pure spiritual teaching could be brought to the human world in the form of a book, it would lose its purity the moment it went through the mind of the first human being who read it.

Remember, what I say is not an opinion of the human world or indeed the human mind, no, it is only an observation from a higher perspective; in the same way a teacher can look down on his children in his class and see where they are and know how best to guide them.

To all of you I say, try and be true to yourself on your spiritual path and you will have all the doctrine you need to be your guide through the human journey.

Can faith really affect things in our lives? What is the power of faith and how does it work?

The power of one's faith can indeed change circumstance; it is a part of your make-up which can shape your will, and when your will has direction or intention it becomes a driving force that can move things, or even attract things towards you. Faith is like the wind that forces the sails on a ship and moves it forward. Your attitude is like the sail; when limp it becomes motionless with no real direction or intention. But when accompanied with faith as its driving force, it can carry you to where you need to travel in your life with much ease. But like the wind, it comes and goes, therefore you must make good when you have faith behind you.

There are those whose faith is strong and they do stand out as great figures among people in the human world, but they are few among the many. This type of faithful person may encourage others to share their faith, but I say to you now, the faith that comes from self is the strongest and most important. Remember, faith can be built upon, like the wind it can pass through you, so you must ready yourself when you can and expand your attitude in preparation to catch the wind.

Are religious people more likely to gravitate to a higher level in the after-life than atheists?

People are people, the term religious being added to them does not necessarily make a person more spiritual, more wise, nor compassionate; these virtues are gained by how you have lived and understood your life.

There are many who follow the law of a religion in your world and grow spiritually because of it. People such as this have obviously taken the more spiritual values suggested within its teaching, but I suggest to you that such people are open spiritually and would grow the same way, no matter what banner they chose to learn under.

You use an interesting way to describe the ascension of the human spirit through the spirit world by talking of gravitation. This is quite precise and the mind that is clear will move higher than the mind that is clouded, confused or ignorant of their previous actions.

The highest religious state a man can achieve is when he has felt goodness fill his being through acts of kindness or compassion; let this be the start of your own religious doctrine and build on it through the rest of your journey.

Who really hears our prayers? And is it important to have a prayer life?

The spirit world hear your prayers, your thoughts, and senses your inner feelings, so know that when you go into silent contemplation and ask for help or guides for yourself, or others you care about, your communication is always received.

The human prayer is interesting because it is often the most honest communication a person makes, especially when it comes from the heart of him. It is through the act of praying that your mind opens to the possibility of a higher being and therefore you are, by your action, acknowledging that.

Of all the many prayers you send out into the ether, only some will be rewarded, but even if you find that one has been answered in a favourable way to you it will form a belief, and when you first begin to believe, then you are ready to start to trust. For this reason alone, and there are many others, it is good for you all to have a strong prayer life.

Take a moment, if you will, to consider some of the ways praying to a higher power can help shape your mind to a more positive state.

The first thing to consider is it opens you to search for compassion for other people who may be less fortunate than you are. To care for others in this way is the beginning of the awakening of a spiritual life.

There is also the acceptance you may learn when the prayers you have sent out are unanswered or not rewarded, but a realization in you teaches you that the higher power allowed life to take its own action without divine intervention. There is also the matter of your own higher consciousness coming into the equation; in the silence of your own mind is where you meet yourself spiritually, and because of this, you have access to the world of higher powers.

Yes, it is very important for all of you to pray when you can, but remember to guide your prayers in a way that they might be realized, and also know that not everything you ask for can be done.

Try when you can to use prayer in a positive manner and when you feel strong spiritually, remember you too can send good will and intention to others from your own spirit.

Do you have a better understanding of God when you are in the spirit world?

The first thing you will gain is a better understanding of self and from this you would obviously have more of an understanding of the higher force. There are many changes that take place when you return home to the spirit world, but there is much dissolving of the recent human existence which has to occur and when it gradually fades, the lighter and brighter the consciousness becomes.

Only in a state of lightness can you absorb more of your own true identity and thus the realization of what you refer to as God.

Are there states of spiritual ascendency like nirvana?

There are no limits to the clear mind and such states can be achieved if aimed towards. Before you look to such risen states of mind in the spirit world, try to aim your mind towards the highest and best clear state of mind that you can achieve in the human world. Once again, I remind you that you are as limited as you allow yourself to be at the moment.

Strive for the highest and you will at least get a better perspective of your existence, dream of it and you will sometime have to wake up; therefore, the effort you put into it will determine how high you can go in this world, or any world for that matter.

Remember, there are those who even in the human body have raised their consciousness to the clear states in the spirit world, so it can be achieved from where you are now.

Is there any common link between all the world religions?

Yes, they are all filled with people. Once again, I tell you that the aim or intention of what you term 'religion' is to make people evolve spiritually, but the people who minister the teachings have to understand spirituality at a higher level to truly have a chance of enlightening the minds of their followers. By this I mean that the teaching is just a teaching, remember it still has to be realized to have an effect and the outcome of the effect will depend much on the teacher.

Is it not true that in all of your religions there are teachings of goodness, kindness, healing and hope? These virtues are the thread that runs through all of these spiritual teachings, but it is not the good of the religion that is damaging. No, it is more to do with the controlling factors and manipulating tactics they hold over man that makes them negative and causes them to fail to enlighten on a more spiritual level. Remember, there is one force of life and you are all a part of it, no matter how your mind chooses to believe in it.

Is religion dying in this world and will it eventually cease to exist all together?

Would I be right in assuming that once again I am being called upon to predict the future in the human world? No, such a question has no answer that would help you grow at this time, so instead, if you allow me, I will talk to you of change.

You will have noticed, at this point in your lives, many things that were in your life are no longer there, yes? Now if you look at the bigger picture and survey the history of the human world and what you know of its evolution till now, you will again be made aware of things that once were a part of the human journey and are no longer a part of it; is this not so, also? Then, wouldn't it be safe to make the assumption that at some point the mind of man will evolve and have better and much clearer understanding of what is termed 'religion' in his world?

Even in the here and now, the way some people think of religion is so far removed from how it was thought of a thousand years ago, and from this we may be so presumptuous as to say that it will follow in this pattern until it is no longer required as a teaching of spiritual growth in the human world.

If religion in the human worlds dies out, it will be because of the expansion of the mind of man.

Is there any connection between God and those people on earth like the Pope and

archbishops, who are chosen holy people? Or is it the same connection for us all?

My young friend, you have answered your question in its second part. If you look at God as being an individual and in some ways like the top figure, you may be tempted to think that His representatives on Earth would form a pecking order depending on who is allowed to wear the biggest hat, all the way down to the one who must shave off all his hair; now I jest with you, my friend.

But the role of spiritual leader on Earth is not a God-given office, if you like, but decided upon by man himself. Therefore, the man who acts as spiritual ambassador is not necessarily more spiritual that the humble man who practises good deeds and lives his life with loving intentions.

Summary

I am not sure when I read the previous answers if Chi's thinking has shaped my own mind or if we are connected spiritually because we have similar considerations and understanding, because as far as I can remember, I have always thought that people can be very spiritual without being very religious.

In my early life, my parents never followed any religion and there were never any religious teachings opened to me other than in my early school days, and back then we were only taught about Christianity based on the Church of Scotland. Yet as a small child I used to often pray for people and I always knew that there were spirits around me who could hear my prayers. As young as eight or nine, I believed I could heal people with my thoughts, which sounds quite crazy even now as I write these words, but I genuinely thought that my prayers were made of powerful stuff and that someone out there was helping me.

I have definitely done my research into different religions during my life and have been fascinated by all of them, but never pulled in to join any. I think this is because I have always known that I would follow an individual path and one that could be open to all teachings, and hopefully connect to them, too.

Over the years, Chi has answered so many questions on religion during our trance sessions, from people asking about how God came into existence, to where they could find the Holy Grail.

I believe, for me, the best question that he answered was when someone asked him if God was a woman and he answered that she could not be – otherwise she would never have created man.

This type of response makes people laugh and it shows that there is an authentic personality coming through. On the same question, he did give a very interesting answer after the laughter subsided, when he told the group that it would make more sense to assume that the giver of life was feminine, rather than masculine, but that consciousness at this evolvement would be both and none at the same time, and that to us it should not matter until we were ready to understand it.

That was many years ago and since then I have a little more understanding of it, but that will have to keep for another time; you see, now I am starting to sound like Chi.

8

Healing

Introduction

I believe that healing is very important to anyone who is on a spiritual journey. I am so glad that my old teacher, Mrs Primrose, made me study healing for several years before she allowed me to move on to mediumship. I think that during my time in the healing clinic, I learned much more about people's needs and their hurts than I could have ever done from most other places or situations in my life.

I have met and worked with so many amazing healers during my life, and it gives me great hope to know that there is another force in the world we can call on when all else fails. I believe it is a life-force, and that there is life all around us and not just in us. When a person is open in a spiritual way, they can harness more of life's energy; it can be drawn down from the atmosphere and channelled through such a person. I think that spiritual healing in any form is a God-given gift. It works mainly through our compassionate nature and shows the human spirit at its best, wanting to give to others.

Healing is highlighted in many spiritual teachings and the Bible is filled with remarkable accounts of miraculous healing being done on the suffering. It is a great place to start your spiritual journey, because all you need to do is find compassion for others and, before long, something good will begin to change in you.

I love when people ask Chi about healing, because he is always so clear in his answers; even when the questions seem complicated or confused, he always finds a way to simplify them. In this next session, there were so many questions of a personal nature, relating to their own illnesses, that we could not put them all in. Instead we have used those questions that might have a wider appeal, for people who have an interest in the subject and need answers about how it works and on what levels.

How does Spirit see the scientific, modern, approach to medicine and therapies versus traditional and nature-oriented healing methods? Is there an antagonism, with so many people still in each camp, or a way to use the best of both worlds?

Much of what you see in the human world of scientific progression in medicine, or otherwise, comes into your world because it is brought there by a mind that intended to do so as part of his or her contract. So it becomes relevant in its proper time and the only mystery in this would be if the inventor or creator has forgotten that they were actually meant to discover this or that breakthrough. With this in mind, you might understand your question better before I continue to answer the next part.

If all medicine is relevant and its practitioners are sincere and learned in their field, then all form the basis for healing. It is difficult to be more exact as your question is open and very general. So I must say that if there is antagonism, it would only be experienced in the human world; Spirit have no use for antagonism.

The second part of your question deals with using both methods where it is possible and that is always advantageous to the healer and indeed to the practitioner, as it will open both their minds to the other's healing technique and in some cases cause further advancement in new healing formulas, and so on.

Always remember this, there is a limit to how much the human body and mind can be healed and there is always a time for the correct healing to take place, if it is to be. Therefore, always remember the core of any healing practice and that is compassion.

How should an individual make a good decision, if and when they are confronted with a serious disease and have choices to make?

This is a strange way to put a question, for in one sense you are asking about the individual, yet you expect an answer to be general that would fit all. If I may suggest to you, my friend, that what you are asking would almost certainly have a different outcome for each person who is faced with such a condition in their life, then maybe you will understand that it would be impossible to form any kind of accurate answer.

If you will allow me to talk to you for a moment about choice in the human world, then maybe an answer will form that will give you more clarity on the matter.

When the body becomes ill or infected with disease, as you say, then a person has a choice to try various methods to bring about healing where it is possible.

Now each illness may have a different effect on different individuals and, of course, there may even be various strains of disease that will add more complications in some situations. Take into this equation that there is also the destiny of the individual's life to be considered and that some individuals die from non-threatening illness, while some live on through what was supposed to be incurable, is this not so? With this in mind, you must try to understand that there are often more things playing out than what is simply in front of you, when it comes to the human life.

But in its simplest form, the right healing is the one that has the best results, even if that means a mixture of all things.

Does Spirit sometimes recommend specific healing modalities, like through Edgar Cayce?

Remember, Spirit can guide and sometimes advise you, but we can never live your life for you. By this I mean that we can help by leading you towards solutions, but to recommend one would be like an endorsement of something which is not necessarily perfect in its entirety and would then mean that, even as good as it has been for some to use it, it would never heal all people with all illnesses; especially when hope is exhausted and the life is about to be over.

The medium you mention, Mr Cayce, the work he did was relevant for his time to open the minds of certain people to the possibilities of higher knowledge, but even then his work was not all accomplishing, as it was in the human world, where there is an abundance of illness, infections and, of course, death.

I would say to you that when such a practitioner is in your world, you must take from them what suits and what works and also learn from the entire situation and not just the healing aspect. It is important for you to note that the medium was the vehicle that allowed greater medical knowledge to come into this world, at a time when medicine was making great advances, and much of what was channelled was to the medical mind as much as the patient.

Remember, time brings change and much of what

happens before is no longer relevant to the here and now, so you must learn to open your mind and become more aware of what is useful in a realistic way and what is fanciful and without purpose.

How about various quite popular 'new age' methods, like Touch for Health, Reiki, Quantum Healing, Angel Healing, and the like? How about Colour Healing, Bach Flower Remedies, Breathing, Relaxation Techniques, Shamanism, Huna, or Tibetan Pulse Healing?

Healing is healing and many times during your physical journey the body will need repairs and treatments. You mention many types of healing and I am sure that each has an importance to whatever they are all used to fix. But again, I ask you to consider good sense when trying to repair the human body or mind.

One must seek the medical treatment that fits the illness; so if the body has slight damage or mild infection, one does not require the assistance of a consultant doctor, or extreme healer who performs at a very high level. Neither would it need powerful drugs or potions to repair the slight ailment. The same would apply in all the types of healing practices you have mentioned.

The terms you use are just words; it is the person who performs the healing who is important, and the authenticity with which they use their gift or talent.

In the same way, if you know someone to require

the highest of medical treatment, you would not put them in front of a healer who is known for curing warts.

No, be sensible in your choice where you can and remember that most of the healing the human body requires is inside. When you find a way to lift your mind to a higher state, then the body will surely follow.

What about radiation? We are constantly subject to an increasing number of radiation types – mobile phones, electromagnetic sources in computers, electric grids, and so on. Are they possibly a health hazard? Will they influence our consciousness?

There are two answers to this question. One is that there is always a danger to the body from subatomic particles which are, in some way, holding within them radiation and reveal activity. But as the form of the human being adapts and grows, the younger generations of this world shall be less affected by these toxins.

Sadly, those of your generation do not have the same resistance, for you have not the immunity through your parents and through the generations before, who absorbed such poison into the physical world. But this world, by its nature, has become more radioactive, if you like.

The person who has asked me this question did not just mean radioactivity, but radiation by electromagnetic radiation, like from mobile phones, or from electrical currents from electricity, which create a kind of field of electromagnetic things.

Forgive me, I lived on this Earth one thousand five hundred years ago, it takes a moment to try to catch up with technology, but I shall do so. It is the same effect of which I speak.

Within the mechanism that you discuss, there is a form of radioactivity less toxic to the modern people, and so progression and evolution shall allow that the new forms of life on this planet shall not be as affected by such mechanisms. But to the older generation there is, in fact, some threat to health, but it would not alter when they should die. That has already been predetermined, and no phone in the world shall make a change to that.

What is actually happening with the so-called 'psychic healings' through Filipino or Brazilian mediums, sometimes also called 'psychic surgeons', where the body is actually 'opened' and people get cured? Can one explain these phenomena in any way?

One can try. The practice you describe has all the makings of a human ritual and display of force,

rather than spiritual healing. If you have any awareness of Spirit and how they function, you will know
that such a display would be thought of as forceful
and intrusive and has less to do with Spirit than you
may know. Remember, the human mind in its own
right is very powerful and some people have learned
to exercise their mind to create phenomenal circumstances and superhuman happenings.

It would be more reasonable to believe that what
is going on in this type of surgery is base phenomena
and closer to the human world than the spirit world.
You only need remind yourself that Spirit are non-
physical and therefore could penetrate the body with
healing without the patient even being aware of it.

Keep this image in your mind when you think of
spiritual healing in future. The spirit is gentle in all
practice; where there is force, it is of the physical
world, and remember also that not everything you
see is actually happening. Another thing of importance to share with you at this point is to ask yourself what is most important in this subject, the
so-called phenomena, or the healing?

Mother Teresa was criticized sometimes,
because she supposedly did 'nothing' to try
and heal the sick people that she and her
nuns were caring for, and instead just accom-
panied them until they reached the threshold
of passing over from this world into another

*state of existence. Are there times when it
may be more essential simply to be with
someone very sick, in a coma or the like, and
not to try all the various therapies, medicines
and machineries? Asked differently, is
'healing' sometimes not the ultimate goal at
all, but rather being and accepting?*

The word 'accepting' is important when we talk of
healing. It can be the first stage in the healing of
many things, not least the grieving process which
you go through when the loved one passes to the
higher side of life.

Also, the desire to be with the dying is an act of
bravery in your world. The lady you mention was
wise and chose to exercise her wisdom over dying
and death. This comes from one who is spiritually
evolved and knows that struggle will only cause the
mind of the dying person to suffer at an emotional
level, which can be prevented if the person in attend-
ance of the dying person has acceptance in the matter,
and also the mental strength to know that the immi-
nent death is natural and part of life.

There is a time when no treatment will resurrect
the fading life-force and this is when wisdom must
prevail and acceptance be allowed to take over. If
you only knew how aware the dying are of the spirit
world as they pass, and often before their passing,
you would not try to prolong their life a moment
longer than is necessary.

You will learn during the course of your life that sometimes it does more good in a situation to do nothing other than love and care for another, so never underestimate the power of such things; after all, they are two of the major components of pure healing.

How can we heal psychological wounds and traumas, such as being emotionally or physically molested, abused or raped, being dumped or neglected, and so on? How can we deal with emotional healing? Work through and relive the traumas? Forget and go on? Any helpful suggestions by Spirit?

The emotional healing you ask about differs only from the physical healing in that it has to be understood by the mind before it can be released in most cases. Unlike the body, which can be healed and the results will become apparent to the area that was aided as it begins to function normally again, in such a happening the mind will tell the body to start to function as normal.

With emotional episodes, the mind may force them deep into its darkest recesses and hold them prisoner for a long term; therefore, in healing such traumas, the mind must release its secrets to the light side of the mind to be processed and accepted before true healing and release of such heartache can occur.

I have mentioned to you in many answers that

when we talk of the human mind, each one is individual, and as such will progress in their own way and in their own time. There are so many cases when deep emotional traumas are not resolved during a person's lifetime and they will be brought back into the physical world in a future life to be worked out and dissolved.

There is no amount of healing of any type that can force the individual to release their emotional pain; this has to happen when the patient is at a point in their life when they want to be free of it or find understanding of it.

Your own human attitude is a great tool to work on your own emotions. When you realize that through the power of your own mind you can lift your attitude and make the most of the power within you, you have a chance to heal on an emotional level. The human race is so varied and some of you come into this world to live a life of example to others.

How brave are the ones who take on suffering, in order to show others that it can be done. There are so many examples of bravery over suffering throughout the history of mankind and it must be put to good use when it comes to healing the mind. In all forms of emotional healing, whether you are the patient or the healer, remember kindness, to self and to others.

*Sometimes one hears the term 'soul healing'.
How is it from the viewpoint of Spirit? Is the
soul, the individual 'drop of spirit', always
whole and so not in need of any healing, but
just the personality, the ego, and the circumstances the person identifies with? Or can the
soul, the individual spirit, ever be 'sick',
'diseased' and in need of healing?*

You ask so many questions in one that in order for
there to be any sense made of the answer, I shall
have to break them down, if you do not mind, my
friend.

The first thing you ask of is soul healing, is it
not? Then let me say that the word 'soul' is a term
used by man to distinguish a higher part of him.
With this in mind, the higher you travel through
your consciousness, the less chance there is of being
out of balance; so no, the soul, and I assume you
are talking of the spirit or higher consciousness, does
not become sick.

Now try to understand that within your world
there are many terms, words and references to the
higher mind. I hear some of you call it your spirit,
or your soul, or your consciousness. All of these
terms are clearly understood as higher parts of the
being. Try not to get so hung up on terms and decide
which you would rather use, but avoid where you
can dissecting the spirit into many fractions.

It is hard enough for you to understand that you

are a physical being that has a higher life-force without turning that spiritual essence into a multi-divisional being.

So, in simple terms, the higher part of you does not become ill, only the physical and emotional aspects of you, which are affected by your human existence, decay and eventually diminish. So when we think of healing, remember it is impermanent and of use only when required and meant to function; in other words, there is a time for healing.

Summary

Healing is the core of my practice as a medium. I firmly believe that in order to be a good medium you must also be a good healer; after all, the act of mediumship is about taking people who are sad and trying your best to bring happiness back into their lives.

I find it fascinating that the spirit world come and help us to understand and work with healing energy, yet they often talk about the time for healing as being so important. Chi often mentions that healing will only take place when it is the correct time and that it will have the desired effect that it is supposed to.

If this is true, it made me wonder about all the times I gave healing to people when I was learning and if they were just a waste of time. I got one of my circle to ask my guide this the next time he came through in a trance session, and this is what he said:

> All healing is important, even when you think you are not having a positive effect on your patient or curing them of what ails them. It is the practice that lifts your vibration to a more spiritual height in preparation for the next person you are to work on. My medium will understand when I tell you that there is always something going on during the healing sessions he takes part in. The first thing to understand is the exchange of energy between the two people and indeed the spirit world, so something positive is happening even if it is not what you think it is.
>
> The people that came to Gordon in his early days of healing were brought there for him to practise and become more confident in his abilities, in the same way a student of medicine would only be allowed to learn the simplest of things in anatomy before being allowed to take their next step. In his work, others began to approach him with more serious complaints and he was used by Spirit to heal them where it was the right time, but he would not have been able to channel such power without practice, you see. It is so important for you to remind my medium that in healing, where it is true, people may get what they need, but not always what they, or even the healer themselves wants.

On listening back to this statement it did remind me that I am just the vessel in healing, as I am in mediumship, and all I can do is be clear and open to try to do my best for whoever comes for help. Sometimes we are so eager to do good work and help that we forget that there is a power higher than us, who sees much more than we do and who knows the correct procedure to follow; the word 'trust' comes to my mind, just trust.

9

On Love and Loving

Introduction

There have been so many sessions where people have asked questions of the spirit guides about love. Mostly, people want to know about relationships when they ask about love and that is all right, because so many people find that the highest love they have experienced in this life is when they have felt love with another person.

I remember on one occasion, when a woman asked my guide if she would be judged because she was married in the eyes of God, but had three lovers whom she loved equally and could not give up. The answer came back:

> Madam, for what would you be judged, on your infidelity or your lovemaking? It would seem that judgement would have no effect on changing what you do, would it?

She replied, 'No, because I love myself and all the men I'm involved with, so I'll just go on as I am.'

I still laugh out loud when I read the transcript

of this trance session, but my guide always reminds us that it takes all sorts to make up this human world.

Is it important to love, or be loved, in this life? Can you explain love?

Let me begin by answering the last part of your question first, if I may. You ask if I can explain love; well, this is one of the most difficult things that I would have to put into words for you, my friend. At its simplest, it is a force, a power which is constant throughout realms of life. Love is in you and in all living beings. To some it is apparent and others it is not, but it is ever present where there is life. For now, it would be wise to keep it this simple.

Is it important to love or be loved in your human life? The answer to this is yes. It is so very important for you to know that you are loved first; this is emanated from your mother the moment you are born and from the father the moment his eyes look upon his child for the first time.

The force of this unseen power is what connects the parents to their offspring and is the first offering of unseen energy that binds them together in the initial stages of their togetherness.

The innocence of the child in this situation brings forth feelings in the parents of care and compassion, protection and need to nurture, all of these will only strengthen the bond of love between them. So from your earliest entry into this world you should experience what it feels like to be loved; something you will wish more of for most of the journey of your human life thereafter.

Having experienced love in your human life, you will try to love back, as love by its nature is an essence which flows, and is easier to recognize when it is given and reciprocated at one and the same moment by two people. The importance of loving or being loved is to know, even if only for a moment, the experience of life when love is more present than not.

Try for one moment to imagine the newborn who enters this world and is not loved immediately; where love is absent, fear will take over. This may help you to understand some of the cases of human behaviour which take place and are deemed to be horrendous; such bad behaviour comes from a heart filled with fear and lacking in love. So now you may understand why it is important for the human being to love and be loved.

Is it predestined for us to find love in this life?

In some ways it is indeed predestined for you to find love or reconnect with those who are open to the love you have in you. I believe though, my friend, that you are talking about partnering, rather than love of parents and maybe friends, are you not?

Yes.

Then in many cases it is in the contract that you will meet and become partnered with certain individuals during your time in the human world. There may be experiences of love in such unions, but it is also often that such episodes are created for both parties to gain new sensations and experiences and thus it is not always that predestined meetings are long lasting. The wise among you will preorder such a meeting near the end of the human time, so that you will both follow one another back to the spirit world and bring with you the bond of human love.

In truth, there are so many different scenarios when it comes to human love and the many ways it is played out. In each life the individual will gain much from the acknowledgement of the existence of love in their lifetime. There is more to speak about in this matter, but I feel to do so might answer some of the other questions which others have to ask in this session.

Is there such a thing as a soul mate and, if so, does everyone have a soul mate, even if sometimes it feels as if they do not have one?

And now I am answering my own questions, my friends, for this was what I was about to speak to you of, the term so often used among you today, 'soul mate'. Yes indeed, there are some who feel that the love is deep between them and would assume that such love is above the human world and the limited time they would spend together in it.

They would be right, as any precious love is bigger than the human existence and will outlive it, because love, unlike the human life, is able to move through time; it is not of it, and it will continue beyond what your limited mind can imagine, and may even be the cause of opening up your mental and emotional horizons and expanding your mind and capacity to understand more.

But remember this, all of you are able to do this of your own accord without the assistance of another. From the human perception, it would sometimes appear that a deep human love is the greatest thing you can experience and for many it is, but each of you has the capacity to love, in the same way as two people who claim that their spirits are matched and perfectly designed to accompany one another through all eternity.

Such deep love in humans often becomes exaggerated to the point of being heavenly, but this is due to the human emotions being pushed beyond boundaries never even imagined before. Love will always be bigger than the lover and must be recognized for what it is.

Do not allow your human emotions to run away with you when it comes to love; be wise and know that all the love you require is in you.

Why is it that some people can love someone and then lose that love for them. Why doesn't love last forever?

My friend, love is the constant in life, people are impermanent; more than this, the feelings of the human being change more frequently than the weather around the planet. Remember, to feel love, something rises in you and your heart lifts to a higher state of being.

It is in this heightened state that you can meet love and let it into your heart. At this point it can be given from one heart to another. When this occurs people feel different and often have no idea how best to express their heightened experience. Even the poet or the artist finds it difficult to contain love within the words on a page or paint on canvas.

Is it not so that during this in-love type of experience a human mind is not its normal functioning self? Would it not be fair to say to you that the human being in love is in an altered state of consciousness, almost like a semi-trance state?

There are so many ways to interpret love in the human world and only when it becomes difficult to put into words are you close to the real thing; for love is above you in purity and has to be reached only by the heart that is elevated, by such expressions as compassion and great yearnings to give for the sake of true advancement. Simply, when you feel it, cherish it, open your heart to it, but respect it and it will pass your way again.

Is it possible that we might fall in love with the same person in every reincarnation and just not remember it?

If this were so, then there would indeed be much to learn for both involved. I say this to you because it would not be very enlightening to constantly repeat the same experience time after time without progression to follow.

Again, this is a human ideal, based on the human emotional attachment you form with certain people during a lifetime. Yet would it surprise you to know that you have felt the same in each lifetime, only with a different person? If this were the case, would it not be apparent to you that the lesson which was not being absorbed was the actual forming of attachment and not the everlasting love for the other individual?

Children of the Earth plane, it is understandable that you want to hold onto your love forever, and let me assure you that you will, but not in the way your limited human mind perceives this to be.

No, you must be open to love and follow what lessons come to you with that episode. Just trust me when I say that love above the human mind is much more expansive than any of you can know at this time; but all of you do know this at a more spiritual level and I know that even as I speak to you of this, my words will help you reach up to the higher notion and let it rest upon your mind for a moment.

The simplest thing I could say to you concerning

love at this time would be that you mustn't struggle when love is with you, just let it be.

Do we always find the people we have loved when we go into the spirit world?

Yes, is the short answer to your question, but I have come to learn that you want more of the technical elements when it comes to these answers.

It is important for those who are coming back to the spirit world to know that their physical existence is at an end, and the simplest way to make this as gentle a transition as possible is for those whom they know to be in the spirit world to be waiting for them, to bring them into the higher state of being. Also, there is an element of adjustment which has to take place and it involves the spirits that are already in the spirit world helping to raise the vibration of the one who is returning.

Much of what I say to you now may sound very like a welcoming committee on the Earth plane, but there is much more going on at a higher level than I can describe to you, so for the purpose of answering this question, I will leave it as such.

Many spiritual teachings say we must learn to love one another, but how can we learn to love someone who is bad to us, or cruel to people we love?

I think it would be easier for you to try to love them more, than to have to love them more. You are not lord over love, but you do have control over your own mind and your attitude. In the case where someone has wronged you, you may not be able to find deep love for them, but if you can open your heart and mind and try to understand the reason for their bad behaviour, then a positive change will occur in you. This type of change of heart may bring about a change of mind and, if such occurs, then the seeds of love have been sown.

Some of the teachings in the human world are very direct and do not leave much room for adjustment or consideration, but I say to you, take all teachings at a level that you can understand them and when you cannot, let it be, until you feel ready to revisit them with a fresh approach. Do not think for a moment that you should have to accomplish all spiritual teaching in one lifetime, as this would be impossible for anyone to do.

It is difficult for you to take in the fact that people who hurt others, or behave inappropriately in your world, can be loved by others or should deserve any kind of compassion, but think this way for a moment. If there were not those who chose to come to your world to perpetrate bad actions, how would the masses that learn from it actually learn?

Again I say to you, try to understand that which makes you feel at peace and balanced and leave that which disturbs you for now. Love those you love to the best of your ability and you are truly helping your world.

Is the love we feel for each other in the physical world experienced the same in the spirit world, or is it different?

Love is love, my friend, it is always the same no matter where, but the individual differs in their expression, that is all. The only thing I wish to add at this point is that it is easier to love in the higher world, because love is more easily understood, and it is also in abundance and part of the very atmosphere, if I can say this. But there are those in the human world who lift their minds to such a state of bliss that they break through barriers and taste the heights of the spirit world, while being still grounded on this Earth.

If a life partner dies and their other half finds new love, how is the spirit partner affected? And will they all meet in the after-life?

This is a good question and one which I am sure is appropriate to you, madam. I feel that you have indeed lost a husband to the spirit world and that you have since found love again to share your life? I am not at this moment bound to give to you a message from your first husband, but I will tell you this. He is so happy that you have found love again and, in fact, says that he was responsible for guiding you towards meeting your new husband, and therefore it pleases him no end that you loved him enough that you trust he will always love you, no matter what. Is this not so, madam?

Yes, this is so.

Would it now surprise you to know that, before any of you came to this human world, you all made this contract together as you are all part of the same unit of loving beings who chose to work and grow together?

No, it would not surprise me.

Then, madam, you have your answer and I hope it will help to bring clarity to others who are listening at this moment. Oh, and just before we move on, George says that he thanks you and your new partner for bringing flowers to his place of rest last week. I know I said that I would not give you a message, madam, but sometimes things change.

Can the feeling of love in our life help us, or when we are in love, do we grow spiritually because of love?

I would say to you that you grow more lovingly than spiritually, but in some ways you will grow spiritually if you learn the lessons which are involved in your loving relationships. Remember, not all loving relationships last for the term of your human life, many bring great heartache and sorrow. Such endings are not there to punish the individual, but to teach the value of life when love is present, against the times when it is not. Is this understood?

The entire group replied with affirmation.

Try to think like this for a moment. Your human life is like a tool to use in order to grow in spiritual ways. Why is this so? It is so because the lesser, more contained human life can be watched over and learned from by the higher spirit. Things like emotion and suffering can be observed and learned from and wisdom can be achieved as a result.

I have spoken much about compassion in this session, but we must also remember that wisdom is also a part of love and especially when one has wisdom, then they know how to love appropriately.

Sometimes there are 'love triangles' and many questions and doubts come up. Do you have any insight on that?

Sometimes your human emotions cause such a tangle, like a web around people who practise certain practices, and yet have fear that their practices are not always wholesome to the other people they affect.

Damage, gentleman, can only be done to a third

party if the third party is aware of it in this world. The ongoing result shall be that, of course, they shall notice when they enter the spirit world, but then would it not be so that they also knew this when they came to this world and made the contract with the person they are now with?

All of these actions are human behaviour, neither right nor wrong, until they have caused torment. They cannot cause torment if they are not known. Do you understand this?

Yes, that answers it fully.

Summary

During the many sessions in which I have taken part, so many people have been given answers to questions regarding their love lives, and love in general, for that matter. I believe that it is something that will always cause us to question, because of the nature of love itself, and no matter how many answers we get, or books of philosophy we read, the individual will always demand an individual answer and not imagine their love to be so general that it can have simple solutions that might suit all.

The one thing that is plain to me in all the answers which Spirit bring to us on this subject, is they constantly talk of love in a way that it is much higher than anything we can know it to be in our human lifetime.

The other thing which becomes quite apparent is how they refer to love as being constant and that we are the ones who need to look for it, rather than expect it to come to our call. Whatever you think of love and whatever you have felt of love in your life, I just thank God that it is out there, and when we are very lucky, in here.

On the Challenges of Our Times

Introduction

These are very challenging times we live in, where so many things are uncertain and not much hope of positive change is given for the near future.

Most of these next questions were asked in more recent sessions and have some connection to the current time and situations we find ourselves in. As ever, Spirit seem to field these questions with ease and no sense of concern; it feels as if they already know what is going to happen, long before we do.

I am often asked if I consult the spirit guides when I have problems or fears in my life and it is difficult for people to believe that I actually do not. Maybe because I have read and listened to so many of these sessions and have learned already from the answers that most of our life we have to get on with things and try to take responsibility for what we do ourselves. The other reason is that I feel it is not always good to know the outcome of a situation, before you have a chance to have the experience of it. This is the typical teaching from Chi and the other spirit guides who work with me.

If awakening and ascension is so great and wonderful, then why is there such a fear to go for it?

To put it into two words, human conditioning.

If you think about it, you have come from a spiritual state which is huge and open into a world that is tight and confined, and which you have become comfortable and safe in. If you are asked to open up and expand into a state of mind that breaks your human boundaries and leads you to have to trust in what seems like an unknown, unseen commodity, then you will encounter fear.

It is natural for anyone in the material world to feel fear when they first begin to expand their mental and emotional capacity. To experience knowing in a way that is not just your brain taking in information, but the heart of you realizing it, is amazing to you and also overwhelming at first. This is completely understandable.

The spiritual student on the Earth plane is preparing to lighten his mind to a point where what was his human conditioning in logic and reality will soon be turned on its head, as the new possibilities begin to build in his deeper contemplations and meditations.

This is why it takes a long time for the development

of the human mind in the matters of spiritual progression, and things like fear and distrust will be experienced, before understanding and awakening reveal themselves to you.

How is it that there seem to be very few really fulfilling encounters and relationships possible and existing in our contemporary phase of awakening and self-realization or 'ascension'?

In each lifetime you choose to take in the human world, there can only be limited experiences of a higher nature. Think for a moment of how limited you are as human beings and how ill prepared you are for the higher energies.

Remember, the spirit world is always around you and coexists with you, but you have not always the capacity to receive our messages or signals; nor in your limited state of mind are you able to sustain what spiritual experiences you actually encounter for more than what is just a moment of your time.

The human reality you live in will always counter any sense of wonderment or higher notion and make it fanciful in the cold light of your everyday awakening. Be patient and honour the spiritual ascensions when they come into your life. Do not be in a rush to jump forward to the next until you have absorbed and truly understood what has actually occurred, and its effects on your life and progression.

Many of us who try to evolve spiritually are experiencing this process as very taxing and some of us have to endure horrid experiences. Will the next generation be 'better off' because we have kind of cleared the way for them, at least a bit?

First, let me point out to you that you do not experience difficulties because you are on a spiritual journey. What may happen is that they become more apparent to you than if you were more ignorant and could not feel the effects of your hardship, as some do not because they are not so aware. Also, the taxing you talk of is part of the human journey, made to seem heavier often when your mind is rising more to the spiritual way of thinking. In your world, it is often thought that if you are good then only good things will happen in your life; this is not so, as I'm sure you already know.

But the mind that is opening spiritually is prepared for such and begins to learn that the difficulties are lessons from which to learn, and only when they are truly realized will they disappear for good.

All good action that you perform in your physical world will help those who follow you, but remember, you are not responsible for all actions that happen during the time you walk the Earth, so just take care of what you have been given to work with and all will be well.

Very often the spiritual path in your world is not

filled with rewards and results are not always visible, but be sure that good actions do affect good future steps.

We see that traditional religions and denominations are losing members and still resist real change. What is the future of the Christian churches like the Catholic, Protestant, and Anglican?

The future of any family in your world truly depends on the children and how they are governed, guided and advised. How they are cared for and nurtured, what they are taught about love and made to understand about fear.

All of this considered, I will invite you to make up your own mind and form a decision about the question which you have put to me, my friend.

I could tell you that when love leaves and fear takes over, then there will be a famine of truth and that without truth how can a teaching survive, but I feel from your question that you wish me to give you an indication of time and this, my friend, I cannot do.

Not because I don't want to, but it would not be right to do so, especially considering you have no real interest or connection to the said church, in ways that the information would be beneficial to you or the organizations themselves. Nor would it benefit anyone else gathered here today to know this.

Should we try to stay in our denomination and rather change it from 'inside', or does it make more sense to leave when the structures and behaviour patterns of the clergy do not fit anymore?

The simple answer to this question is that you must do what your heart tells you to do in situations like this.

To ask another would mean that you have not learned much of your own spiritual being in such matters. The student who needs to follow a religion will be guided by its doctrine, which is dealt out by its chosen preachers. If the student questions the teachings, or indeed the structure of the organization, then he must search his heart and mind for direction.

Will we discover 'intelligent life' out in space in our lifetimes? Or will we be visited by 'aliens' and 'spaceships'? How does Spirit see this whole topic in general?

Remember, what you term 'alien' would also see you in the same way, would it not? And could it not be said that the human race and other species on your planet are indeed intelligent life within space?

I have answered this question in so many sessions and to different people with different levels of understanding, my friend; this is why the answer will sometimes differ.

The way Spirit view life in the universe is the same for all life forms. One which lives in a form that exists through a span of time will eventually die of the body required to take it through that life, and its very life-force, or essence, will come to the spirit world. I must say to you also, my friend, it would be more likely that such life forms will discover you, and already have, long before you could even begin to know how to discover them.

Will we witness the application of quantum physics in teletransportation or other scientific breakthroughs?

If you look at how fast your scientific life is advancing, it would be wrong to assume that when what was once fanciful in the human world has now come to be, then many more fanciful science fictions will not also come into being.

Again, to put a time on such things would not be correct, but think of your childhood and see what has arrived in your life that you could not have imagined back then, and now look to the future and add the same amount of time from then till now, and it will give you a small equation of the time scale.

How does Spirit look upon globalization, the growing population worldwide, and issues of

peace, welfare, water, ecology and the like? Or is this an area where Spirit prefers not to comment?

When you ask about globalizing, I must say that this is something which is already happening in your world. It is the effect of the human mind becoming more intelligent that means its quest will be to investigate the entire world, all species and all cultures.

When this type of thinking occurs, it is only a matter of time before your world becomes smaller and much more multi-connected; those who lead your world will want to extend the parts they lead and sometimes this will mean to join with others, or to overtake others. Either way, globalization is what is happening as we speak.

In matters concerning peace, one would only point out once more that this is something difficult for all of mankind to achieve until there is more of a balance among the ascended mind of the human being; as long as there is great separation between higher and lower in your world, peace will remain beyond the great divide.

When it comes to your ecology and the natural elements like water, my friend, you have all the power within your world right now to make good with such natural substances.

Remember, the Earth was alive before man and she has always found ways to repair herself, and think like this for a moment, does man sustain the planet, or does she sustain the life of all who live on her?

On a more individual level, life seems to be ever more regulated with smoking, driving, airplane boarding, and so on. Will we have to brace ourselves against even more restrictions of individual living? How can we deal with it in a good manner?

All of that you mention is in regard to how men in power choose to legislate over others. Is it not so that most of mankind would prefer to be ruled rather than rule, to be organized rather than take the responsibility of making decisions for themselves? If this is so, then you live in a world that you chose, because you are not ready to make change.

But the way to deal with restriction and discipline is to keep balance and contentment in your own mind; by this I suggest that you consider you have asked for all of these conditions as a lesson to learn from.

Like all lessons, you must try your best to succeed. To succeed when heavily regulated is to bow before them and carry on unaffected. See your mind in this situation as your precious jewel, which needs at all times to be calm and steady, therefore the fight you must fight is the one to keep calm.

*Is there such a thing as cosmic ordering? Can
we ask the forces of the universe for assistance in our life and will they come to us?*

This is a very material way of looking at a spiritual
force, my friend. There are so many ways you can
be given assistance on your human journey and so
many things you could use yourselves to assist others
in their human plight, those less fortunate than you.

It seems that if such a system were available to
mankind, he would use it to make his human life
perfect and thus make useless the human experience.
Such thinking comes from fear, my friend. The true
pioneer of spiritual development and furtherment
of self will endure and learn from the experience,
with little thought of self.

This type of wishful thinking is for the teenager
who dreams and aspires for things in the future,
someone who is not totally immersed in the harsh
reality of human life. Such a mind is like the magi-
cian who wants to know the secret of eternal life
and the forces of the universe at a higher level, yet
his best and most highest desire is not to do good
for the masses with such power, no, his deepest
desire is to turn base metal into gold.

What does this type of thinking tell you, my young
friends? To all of you, I say this. You have made a
contract to come into this life and what occurs during
it are the conditions which you set yourself, in order
to learn and grow in a more spiritual way. Some of

you have bravely chosen to make your journey hard, but know that this will lead to an easier next life; you are the spiritual warriors, because your hardships will teach and inspire others in your world.

Some of you do not fully understand your journey thus far and this, too, is fine as you will soon reach the cusp of understanding, because you have put yourself on the right path to be enlightened, it would seem.

It would be all too easy if the universal powers would erase all suffering from the human world, create world peace, and bring an end to poverty and crime. If we could rid your world of hatred, jealousy, lust for power and greed, then what would be left for you to learn from?

No, my friends, the higher powers cannot change your world because you ask it. We watch over you like a parent watches his child go to school on the first day, knowing we would like to help, but all we can do is be there and reassure you that all will be well.

I say to you now, if a person can promise you gifts from the universe, ask yourself what price you will have to pay at a later time.

Summary

There have been many questions about current-day issues and world affairs during our sessions, but

Spirit always seem to show us that we have to take responsibility for this world and the things we do and say in it.

I suppose when people attend such a session they are looking for answers that will make their life much easier, and maybe allow them not to have to take such responsibility, but it would seem that there is nothing doing on that one.

There is always at least one person who will ask if they can get answers to their own personal problems during the trance. Sometimes Spirit will accommodate and other times they will insist that it is not wise to bring answers forward at that time, as it would not actually do the person much good to know an outcome, but on more occasions than not, some kind of assistance is offered.

Here is one such situation, when someone asked the guide about his son, who was off fighting in the Gulf War in Iraq in 1990–91.

The man asked my guide if he could please help him. There was something in his voice, a deep-seated fear, which made all our attention turn to him. There were about twenty people, including myself, in this small room at the back of a Spiritualist church in south-west England where the session was being held, and everything stopped at the sound of the desperate words.

Listening to this old recording now, it seems so long ago, and in fact it was one of the first times my guide had come through in a trance session, but what came next was very relevant to all of us, not just the man who asked the question.

There was a pause for a moment after the man spoke and then Chi began to speak directly to him:

> Gentleman, I do sense what you are about to ask and I have the permission to give you what you require at this time. Your son will be fine. He will contact you personally in the first week of March of next year and will be sitting in your home with all of his family in the month of May.
>
> Now, because this is information of the future, you may still be very uncertain as to what I say, so I have been told that in order to give you more confidence in what I say, I will tell you his name is Stephen and his birthday will fall in one week's time, while he will be abroad fighting for his country.
>
> Take note of what I say, for it is not the way of the Spirit to give false hope, the only way I can be certain is because he is on a timeline which I am allowed to see. Take this news to your family and no one else and all will be well, blessing to you.

It pleases me no end to inform you that I was contacted by the man early in March the following year, when it had not long been announced that the war had ended, and he was told that his son Stephen was due to be home with his family in May of that year. He was unharmed and had come through the conflict without any bad effects, it seemed.

It is answers like this one that gives me great trust in Master Chi and my other spirit guides and the teaching they bring to us. I know that they cannot do everything for us and lead our life for us, but having them above us does make life much easier.

Afterword

The teachings of Spirit are very simple and often to the point. I believe that many of the answers in this book will be useful to those who seek the truth of spiritual existence and who want to expand their mind to embrace much higher understandings of life as we know it.

To all who took the time to read this, I would say, listen to what has been said and try not to add or take away from it, as most often the words which were given were done so with great purpose and deliberation.

In my many years working with Spirit, I have only ever known them to be compassionate and wise and everything that they take the time to give us is precious to our life's journey. With that in mind, I would ask you to use the teachings brought by Spirit in this book and learn from them what you can, leave what you cannot accept, but do allow it to provoke thought. After all, when we stretch our mind we naturally expand, and expansion is the way of Spirit.

Best wishes,
Gordon Smith

Appendix

Questions not asked and/or not answered

Spirit did not answer all questions presented. Some, especially those on money, politics and the like, were deemed either to be too 'petty' for answers to be given, and any answer Spirit might offer would be subject to dire misunderstandings, hot-air debates, and so on.

Other questions were deemed to open a 'can of worms' and liable to be received as either contradictory or confusing. I would like to quote one example of this. Once in a while, people ask a question about God: 'Does God exist?' Spirit answered this one a few times, but always differently!

Once the answer was:

> Yes, God exists and it makes sense to open up and feel his or her presence and help and grace.

Another time Spirit said:

> No, not really. Actually it is your own spiritual essence which you might want to call 'God' to make it, him, or her more 'objective'.

How come? How can we receive such seemingly contradictory answers? Because everyone is at a different stage of awareness, of awakening and spiritual consciousness. Spirit likes to answer in such a way that the person asking gets the most out of the answer. This means that the answer may be suited to the specific, personal belief system of one person, but it may not suit the spiritual 'make-up' of others.

There is yet another angle to this. The moment Spirit gave an answer that seemed to be absolute on a subject such as God, this answer might be taken up as a dogma. First it might make people more secure in their personality and their spirituality, it might help them to believe, to grow, and so on.

But any dogmatic approach, answer, structure or theory will in the end be confining; it will result in oppression of spirit and freedom and evolution.